Forecasting company profits

Forecasting company profits

FRED WELLINGS

CRC Press
Boca Raton Boston New York Washington, DC

WOODHEAD PUBLISHING LIMITED
Cambridge   England

Published by Woodhead Publishing Limited, Abington Hall, Abington
Cambridge CB1 6AH, England

Published in North and South America by CRC Press LLC, 2000 Corporate Blvd, NW
Boca Raton FL 33431, USA

First published 1998, Woodhead Publishing Ltd and CRC Press LLC
© Fred Wellings, 1998
The author has asserted his moral rights.

British Library Cataloguing in Publication Data
A catalogue record for this book is available from the British Library.

Library of Congress Cataloging in Publication Data
A catalog record for this book is available from the Library of Congress.

Woodhead Publishing ISBN 1 85573 404 4
CRC Press ISBN 0-8493-0517-9
CRC Press order number: WP0517

Cover design by The ColourStudio
Typeset by Euroset, Hampshire, England
Printed by St Edmundsbury Press, Suffolk, England

Contents

v

Contents

Foreword

Profits are one of the integral parts in the valuation of companies. This book should be read not only by those involved in the preparation of forecasts, but also by those who use them. In a world where the corporate business model has become the norm, there is a temptation for the practitioner or student to substitute this for original thinking. An understanding of the dynamics involved in their preparation is more likely to result in a better assessment of their likely outcome and is all part of what the author describes as a well-developed sense of numeracy and a degree of common sense.

Fred Wellings has for many years been a successful and respected analyst and brings his insight to the subject in an enjoyable and informative way. This book is a welcome addition to the literature on corporate valuation and analysis, where books written by practitioners are rare.

Graham Fuller
Chairman, Institute of Investment Management and Research,
1995–97

Acknowledgements

This book has been in progress for longer than I care to admit and my first debt must be to Neil Wenborn of Woodhead Publishing whose quiet support encouraged me to complete a task I might otherwise have abandoned.

I have been greatly helped by colleagues in the investment and business world who devoted considerable time to reading drafts of the book: Christopher Clark, Graham Fuller, Alistair Gibb, Tony Good. Their comments were extensive and have helped to broaden the range of the book. Especial thanks are due to my old friend Sarah Sweetman who read several drafts of the text and helped me prepare many of the theoretical examples. Living within walking distance, Sarah had the misfortune to be interrupted every time I wanted a second opinion or mathematical guidance; without her rigorous examination of the text, many logical inconsistencies would have remained to embarrass me. As always, those mistakes that remain are the author's own responsibility.

The book contains many examples that were first drawn from memory – mine and the readers'. Tracking down chapter and verse is time consuming, and not always straightforward. I am therefore grateful to the many librarians and information officers who helped me with data; particular thanks are due to Rosemary Ackland, the Librarian at Credit Lyonnais Securities.

Introduction

Forecasting Company Profits is intended as a practical guide to forecasting in a commercial environment – the real world where both time and hard facts may be in equally short supply. The book is directed at all those who need to forecast the profits of a company other than their own (i.e. not one for whom they work and that will provide detailed management information); it assumes the forecaster is a third party. In this sense, the forecaster is an outsider – an investor, investment adviser, merchant banker, financial journalist or company executive assessing the prospects for his[1] competitors. Since an essential prerequisite of any profits forecast is the forecast of the appropriate industrial trends, much of the material should also be of relevance to those preparing budgets or involved in industrial forecasting. It may also help finance directors understand how analysts forecast their companies' profits.

The genesis of this book lay in the author's preparation of *Construction Equities: Evaluation and Trading*.[2] The first draft of the chapter on forecasting profits in the construction industry contained blank spaces to await the references to standard works on profits forecasting; alas, no such works could be found or, to be more precise, none that related to the practical experience of 30 years as an investment analyst. There were, of course, books on

1 'He' and 'his' are used throughout the book, but should be read to include 'she' and 'her'.
2 Woodhead Publishing, Cambridge, 1994.

investment that referred to profits forecasting but these often assumed that the forecast had, in the manner of a television cookery programme, been prepared earlier; any description of the actual forecasting process was minimal. There were business books that included sales forecasting techniques for different market structures but rarely integrating that process with the profits forecast; too often, the profits forecasting assumed an insider's knowledge of the company's product mix and cost structure. A typical comment was 'Your credibility as a forecaster is largely tied to how thoroughly you understand the idio-syncracies of your employer's business'.[3] And, finally, there was a class of academic books and articles that varyingly described statistical techniques for extrapolating past trends, but rarely explaining how to judge when such trends may start or finish.

Forecasting Company Profits is unashamedly non-mathematical. Profits forecasting is nothing if not imprecise. The forecaster is handling raw data and economic relationships that may be approximate, or even guessed, while subject to frequent changes in assumptions. It is the author's view that the skills needed to handle such large and changing numerical quantities are not those found in an advanced statistics course; rather, they are the skills and attitudes sometimes described as numeracy and, never to be underestimated, common sense. Of those forecasters that I have worked with over 30 years I saw no evidence that the commercially successful practitioners used any mathematical techniques other than those learned in primary school. What they did have was a well-developed sense of numeracy, an ability to acquire information not generally in the public domain, a shrewd understanding of the inevitability of the business cycle, a belief that what goes up normally comes down, and an ability to challenge received wisdom. Writing in the *Financial Times*[4], Brian Reading pointed to the weakness of economic models but his words apply equally to industry and company models.

'Models cannot handle shocks (like the effects of the Gulf war) or structural change (like German unification). They are not much good at predicting cyclical turning points, either. They assume that what goes up (or down) generally goes on

3   Bails, D G and Peppers, L C, *Business Fluctuations Forecasting Techniques and Applications*, 2nd edn, 1993.
4   20 January 1996.

going up (or down); hence, models regularly fail to forecast recessions or booms until after they are well under way.

'All forecasters massage their results to mitigate these flaws. They change numbers to correspond with their own hunches or to fit in with information not included in the model's equations. But doing this successfully requires a breadth of knowledge and experience which is not obtained simply by being trained to understand and use models.'

Forecasting Company Profits provides an integrated explanation of the theories that underlie the forecasting process, from the industry forecast through to the proverbial 'bottom line', but with a healthy regard for the limitations facing the outsider – not the least of which are lack of information and shortage of time. Although simple models have their place, they are used to provide a framework and to manipulate the data more easily, not as predictive tools. This book prefers to lay emphasis on the patterns of industrial and corporate behaviour and the forecaster's ability to recognise and anticipate these patterns. In that way, he stands a chance of being roughly right rather than precisely wrong. Equally important, the ability to recognise patterns of behaviour allows the forecaster to provide answers when they are required – a commercial requirement invariably overlooked by the textbook. The market does not sleep: share prices respond immediately to events because people are making what they refer to as instant judgements. These judgements are, in reality, instant forecasts and insufficient attention has been paid to the thought process that underlies them.

This book does not suggest what the reader might do with the profits forecast once it has been made. In part, there is an underlying assumption that the objective is already known – much as one does not need to be told the purpose of a book on car maintenance. If there is a temptation to pursue the point and illustrate the varying uses to which the forecast may be put, it swiftly leads into wider issues that can, and do, occupy whole books in their own right. Profit forecasts are rarely made for their own sake but are normally component parts of broader financing and valuation analysis. These end-uses fall into two distinct categories – corporate requirements, where the forecaster has an interest in the totality of the business, and portfolio investment, where the forecaster is valuing shares in the business.

One obvious corporate user of the forecast will be the management of the companies themselves, the 'insiders' referred to earlier. Here the profits forecast will be an integral part of the budgeting process. It will be used for the companies' own planning purposes, for cash flow forecasts, presentations to banks, financial advisers, etc. Companies will also be 'outsiders', making forecasts, explicitly or implicitly, for all those businesses with which they trade (suppliers and customers); for companies that might potentially be acquisitions; and for competitors. Side by side will be financial intermediaries and advisers – accountants, merchant banks, corporate lenders – who will be reviewing companies' forecasts or even participating in the forecasting process themselves.

The portfolio investor is making (or using) profits forecasts as an integral part of valuing shares in the company or, to put it simply, in deciding whether to buy, sell or hold. The share valuation process has its own extensive literature, some generalist, some highly academic. Indeed, there are approaches to share selection (chartism) that do not explicitly incorporate a profits forecast; and investment theories that assume that the market is so efficient that all that can be known is known. Those who do believe, rightly or wrongly, in the relevance of profit forecasting to share selection will still use the forecast in a variety of different ways. It will be used, via a calculation of earnings per share (EPS), to produce a price earnings ratio (PER),[5] the assumption being that the lower the PER, the 'cheaper' the share. The EPS will also indicate the dividend paying capacity of the company and, other things being equal, the higher the prospective dividend yield, the more attractive the share.

Other things are, of course, rarely equal, and simple comparisons of forecast PERs and dividend yields for any given future year are but a starting point. Those forecast ratios need to be judged against the perceived prospects of a company beyond the immediate forecast period; that projected PER will, therefore, depend on the profits outlook that investors are likely to have at that point – and on we go. We move into a world of subjectivity, expectations, emotion, psychology and everything else that makes markets the exciting, frustrating, and occasionally irrational places that they are. It is outside the remit of this book.

5 The number of years it would take for the earnings to equal the share price.

Chapter 1 contains some general observations on the nature of forecasting, warnings and pitfalls, and the philosophy that underlies our approach to forecasting. The rest of Part I covers the industrial background within which the individual companies will operate. Chapter 2, on long term trends, opens with extrapolation; as well as pointing out the dangers, we also provide a rationale for why extrapolation so often works. However, the concern for the forecaster is not the selection and extrapolation of a particular growth rate but the identification of the point when that growth is likely to stop or reverse and this chapter is predominantly concerned with the constraints on growth. Chapter 3 addresses the cyclical fluctuations that exist around the long term trend – from the stock cycle to the capital goods cycle. The objective is to help forecasters understand the nature of the cycles, their hidden peculiarities and, above all, to identify turning points.

Part II of the book moves the forecaster on from the industry to the company. Chapter 4 (market share) provides the bridge between the industry and the specific company profit and loss account. Analysis of potential movements in market share is a particularly judgemental part of the forecasting exercise but we indicate the thought process that should be followed. Before moving on to the detail of the profit forecast itself, Chapter 5 outlines the sources of information available to the forecaster.

In the short term profits forecast (Chapter 6), we construct a simple model with a worked example. We discuss the dynamics of the profits cycle and how managements react, finishing with a section on 'forecasting the unexpected'. Chapter 7 looks at a range of growth companies as they reach maturity to show how such patterns may readily be recognised. The chapter also covers 'the doomsday forecast' and the practice of profits smoothing – essential reading for the forecaster who believes that what happens is always what is published.

Part I

The industry

1 The outsider's challenge

Summary
Chapter 1 comprises a number of introductory comments, the opening premise being that the forecaster does not have access to the management accounts of the company being forecast, nor does he have unlimited time – hence the crucial need for recognising patterns of industrial and corporate behaviour.

We suggest that most people know how to forecast in the sense that they can make judgements about future events; what they lack is the detailed information base and the experience to put events into the appropriate context. We also raise the question 'why do we forecast?'

The chapter concludes with some warnings: the danger of concentrating only on those areas that can be analysed objectively and ignoring those that require subjective judgement; on the danger of model building rather than thinking; and on the fallibility of the raw data on which all forecasters base their projections.

The outsider

The title of this chapter refers to the 'outsider'. Two things characterise the outsider employed to forecast other companies' profits: ignorance and lack of time. Ignorance, in that he possesses a limited knowledge of the background information that would sensibly be considered a prerequisite for successful forecasting;

and lack of time in that the dictates of commercial life, where time is of the essence, rarely allows the forecaster to do all that he knows is possible. That time is a scarce resource is rarely conceded by the textbook or manual, yet, for the practical forecaster operating in a commercial environment, time is a luxury he can rarely enjoy.

To take the time problem to its extreme: the moment the first news flashes appeared after Iraq invaded Kuwait, oil analysts, within the industry and the financial community, were instantly revising their forecasts of the oil price and of company profits; similar instantaneous reaction would be expected from forecasters after, say, a two point panic rise in bank interest rates or a withdrawal of approval for a major pharmaceutical product by the US Food and Drug Administration. There might be a certain intellectual purity in saying that it will take at least a week to come up with a detailed and comprehensive revision of previous forecasts: try that approach in the middle of a dealing room with salesmen trying to create business, or with oil executives wondering whether to cover trading positions, and it is more likely to produce a dismissal notice than a quiet room.

The interesting question then becomes, how is it that analysts, forecasters, commentators – call them what you will – are able to produce almost instantaneous forecasts without having first gone through all the due analytic processes – yet often find that after a week of more considered application and reflection, their first response is left unchanged? Even those who decry 'instant forecasting' do, in practice, adopt a similar thought process when they are users of forecasts. We can all think of times when we have been presented with someone else's heavily documented long term forecast and immediately challenged the conclusions. Implicit within such a challenge to, or disbelief in, another forecast has to be the immediate substitution of an alternative forecast scenario.

Pattern recognition

The simple response to these questions is, of course, 'by drawing on their experience' but the essence of that experience is an ability to recognise a wide range of patterns of economic, industrial and corporate behaviour. The forecaster will have a portfolio of patterns in his mental filing cabinet, even including the exceptional and the unexpected, and it is these he is drawing on when exercising his summary judgement. ▷ **Although this book seeks to provide the rationale for sales and profits behaviour in a variety of business environments, it is particularly concerned to illustrate patterns of behaviour that can be recognised and applied even when the time or the necessary supporting data are not available.** ◁ The emphasis on the recognition of patterns of economic and corporate behaviour is not meant to dissuade forecasters from obtaining a full understanding of the factors that lie behind those patterns. Far from it; that full understanding must be a prerequisite. Nor is it meant to obviate detailed forecasting studies where practicable. Nevertheless, time is limited and not every comment, opinion or forecast can be preceded by days of diligent research. To suggest otherwise is to fly in the face of commercial reality.

There is no intention of suggesting that instant forecasting, for want of a better expression, is anything other than a commercial response to the increasing demands for an instant reaction. In practice, the detailed forecasting studies and the instant response will often sit side by side. While coping with the everyday dictates of the real world, the forecaster will quietly be trying to produce more carefully considered work in his particular sector, to identify changes in trends before they become the consensus view; it is intended that the descriptions of forecasting approaches contained in this book are of as much assistance to the considered as to the instant forecast.

Even those forecasters who abhor the idea of instant forecasting do not have unlimited time in which to choose what areas of their particular market-place will best repay detailed analysis; once again, the awareness of the patterns will help direct the forecaster into those areas most likely to repay the effort. The good forecaster will probably have an awareness of the answer from the beginning. Pursuing the detail allows him to confirm his supposition and to fine tune; it also acts as a basis for explaining and justifying the forecast to the end-user or customer.

No less important than the forecasters themselves are their customers, the people who have to make decisions based on someone else's forecasts. They too will be able to use the patterns and relationships discussed in this book to provide a common sense cross-check to the answers produced by other forecasters' more detailed research. To take a simple example, an understanding of the nature (and even inevitability) of cyclical downturns is a valuable counterweight to the 'this time it will be different' (i.e. there will not be a downturn) school of forecasting which presents five annual profit increases in a row – however detailed the reasoning for uninterrupted growth.

Qualitative or quantitative?

One textbook on forecasting[6] distinguishes between qualitative and quantitative techniques, describing the former as generally reliant on expert opinion or intuitive or informed judgements. Bails and Peppers concentrated on the quantitative or statistical approach 'because the basic techniques are more readily learned, and because the qualitative approach cannot be formalised into a systematic series of steps that are widely applicable to a number of situations. Although expert opinion and judgement are invaluable, they represent the end result of years of study and on-the-job training, which cannot be replicated in a text book.' This view seems to polarise approaches into either the mathematical or the expert, as if they were mutually inconsistent. The 'qualitative' approach is indeed difficult to formalise, as is behaviour in any field, but if that is the way the world works it is of no help to run away from it. It remains only to stress that the forecaster who does not follow a quantitative route is not necessarily innumerate; he may have concluded that quantitative analysis of imperfect data is a delusion.▷ **If one is going to guess the assumptions intelligently and calculate the answer, perhaps one might just guess the answer intelligently.**◁ Aspiring forecasters would also do well to read John Allen Paulos's *Innumeracy Mathematical Illiteracy and its Consequences*,[7] which entertainingly illuminates many of the common ways in which data are misused and misunderstood, saying: 'the book is largely concerned with various inadequacies – a lack of numerical perspective, an exaggerated appreciation for

6   Bails, D G and Peppers, L C, *Business Fluctuations Forecasting Techniques and Applications*, 2nd edn, 1993.
7   Penguin, Harmondsworth, 1990.

meaningless coincidence, a credulous acceptance of pseudo-sciences.'

You already know how to forecast

There is nothing mysterious about the act of forecasting. It is not a strange concept, a trade practised only by those people blessed with a special insight into the future. We all forecast as part of our everyday life – even those sceptics among us who proudly state that they do not believe in forecasting – but we call it by another name. Whenever we travel we make estimates – how long it will take to walk to a meeting, how long a car journey will take; however hedged the response, some estimate is usually made. If the question 'What time are you coming home tonight ?', elicits the response 'Who knows – there is no point in predicting the future', the honest sceptic is likely to receive short shrift. The innate ability to make such a forecast derives from experience of previous journeys, possession of information (e.g. timetables) and awareness of factors that may alter normal expectations (e.g. it is snowing). Time and time again, we return to these criteria – past experience, information and a sense of when things may be different.

▷ **The cornerstone of the forecast is the possession of information combined with the experience to know how to use that** **information.**◁ Information does not have to be formally announced by a company for it to be somewhere in the public domain. At an everyday level, many people are aware which retail organisations are busy and which are losing trade. Locally, it is not necessary to stand outside the factory gate counting the lorries to know whether a company's sales are rising or falling. This is to say no more than there is a wealth of information out there, albeit sporadic in nature, which can be accessed through observation, listening to people, reading local papers or specialist journals, and so on. Valuable though this type of information can be, it is by its nature erratic and there may not be a structured context within which to place the information. It is, therefore, essential to establish the underlying economic nature of the company's business: not just the products themselves but whether they are consumer goods, or capital goods; are they dependent on replacement sales; are the products reaching saturation level; what is the cost structure? To be colloquial, what makes the company tick?

Why do we forecast?

Leaving aside the cynical, but perfectly rational, answer that forecasters are paid to forecast, the conventional response is that if there are events in the future that, were we to know them, would influence our current decision making, then it will pay us to try to forecast those future events, with whatever degree of accuracy can be achieved. As one textbook on economic forecasting put it 'Forecasts are required for two basic reasons: the future is uncertain and the full impact of many decisions taken now is not felt until later. Consequently, accurate predictions of the future improve the efficiency of the decision making process.'[8]

But that is as far as the textbooks go; they give a common sense explanation of why forecasts are needed. However, in a commercial environment, where time equals money, there is a subtler edge to the question 'Why do we forecast?' We may accept the need for forecasting but why are *we* doing it – why not someone else? Often in our everyday lives we use other people's forecasts, timetables being a prime (though not always accurate) example. Sometimes we take other people's forecasts as a basic starting point and then adapt them according to our own needs or requirements – the railway timetable and add half an hour; rain this evening so take an umbrella this afternoon in case. Similarly, in a business environment, it is important to know when to make your own forecast, when to use someone else's (admitting to it or otherwise) or when to take someone else's and modify it. One hesitates to think how many economists there are in industry, the financial world and academia, all making forecasts of the same economic variables. It would be interesting to know how many of the managing directors of firms employing economists actually read the output they pay for and how many draw their views instead from the *Financial Times*, *The Economist* and common sense observation of the world around them. The author has, himself, sat in briefings as one of 40 construction analysts, wondering if the

8   Holden, Peel and Thompson, *Economic Forecasting: An Introduction*, Cambridge, 1990.

world really needs 40 forecasts of Wimpey's profits.

The problem once again is time management. The specialist forecaster is employed to have views on a particular segment of the economy, on the companies within that sector; and to have original ideas. To the extent that you can use already published research, you leave yourself free to do the original work peculiar to your specialisation or employer – either formulating views different from the consensus, or researching an area not previously covered. Using other research does not mean copying competitors' work (who was it that said, 'to copy one person's work is plagiarism, to copy two is research'?) – that is horizontal plagiarism and frowned on – particularly if you are caught. What is to be encouraged is 'vertical copying'. Do you need to prepare your own research on the economy? Do you need to do all the original industry research if there are major studies available, and produced by more authoritative bodies than yourself: The Society of Motor Manufacturers and Traders on motors; Building Material Producers on construction output; or Mintel and *The Economist* Intelligence Unit on virtually anything. ▷**You cannot research everything and it is important to be selective in what you do analyse.** **Save your original thought for interpretation and, always the most satisfying, for challenging the received wisdom.** ◁

Some warnings

The psychological flaw

All forecasting suffers from one inherent psychological flaw and it is shared by all those who write about forecasting. Indeed, it is mirrored across the whole world of social commentary. People feel easiest in describing that which can be given a statistical basis. It is a little like the old army rule: 'If it moves, salute it; if it doesn't, paint it!' Thus, if a topic has statistics available, forecast them; if it does not, ignore it. No better example can be found than the influence of negative equity on the UK housing market after 1989. With a profusion of regional housing sales and price statistics, it was possible to construct a matrix of house buyers who had lost money. However, there were no statistics for the much larger number of people who had been discouraged from buying by what they had observed; so most forecasters ignored the indirect effects and were surprised when the recession lasted far longer than they had expected.

Model building as a substitute for thinking

Model building, by which is meant any consistent framework, provides a disciplined way to forecast; as well as facilitating the calculations. It can also give a professional aura to what might otherwise have appeared no more than a guess. However, model building can also become a substitute for that much more tiring occupation – thinking. The author has all too often seen analysts spending hours, or even days, constructing elaborate spreadsheets to model company profits, unmoved by the fact that there is no reliable data on, say, pricing, or the cost structure. They have worked hard all day, produced a lot of data, successfully avoided thinking and produced nothing of value. The expression 'garbage in, garbage out' is too harsh, but so many forecasters waste their most valuable asset – time – by failing to separate those parts of the forecasting equation where modelling is of value, and those where it adds not one jot to the quality of the answer.

Much of the data needed for effective model building, in a forecasting framework, are difficult to acquire. Just think of the access needed to the cost structure of the companies we are forecasting; or of the resources that go into a full scale industry analysis, and for the multinational companies, this can be replicated for all the overseas economies. If an experienced forecaster is honest, he will occasionally admit to 'guessing' the answer, and working backwards to build up the model. Without seeking to justify such expediency, the skill lies in knowing when that is appropriate, exactly why one is doing it, and what the risks are.

Statistics are often wrong

We now come to another vital health warning. Most forecasting is based on published statistics. For companies, it is company-specific accounting data and for industries it is government or trade statistics. They are the equivalent of the skeleton for the medical profession – not much use in isolation but it is what everything else hangs on. It may come as a disappointment or, indeed, surprise to the novice forecaster that most industry statistics are wrong to varying degrees, sometimes by significant margins. As the *Financial Times* (28/5/96) put it: 'The life of economic forecasters would be a great deal easier if the future was all they had to worry about'. Most experienced forecasters, economic, industrial and corporate, recognise this but try to ignore it – without their skeleton, they are lost.

To paraphrase, all statistics are misleading but some are more misleading than others. Think why. They are collected in a routine way, from people who have more important calls on their time than filling in forms for other people. As you know from your own experience of filling in forms or questionnaires, the definitions you are given do not always fit the circumstances and you have to fudge the answer. If given the form a month later, you may well answer in a different or less consistent manner; your interpretation will almost certainly be different from that of some other form filler. Since drafting this paragraph, I found myself the recipient of the CSO's 'Quarterly inquiries into turnover of the distribution and services sector'. Unable to decide whether I could best describe my one man lifestyle as 'financial services' or 'other activities' I elected for the former on the basis that it required no additional explanations: such are statistics.

The most reliable statistics are normally those that involve a *physical count* of a particular product, such as tonnes of coal dug up, or the number of cars registered in a month. However, just because the statistics are published by an authoritative source does not mean they are correct. In November 1996 the World Bureau of Metal Statistics suggested that there were substantial stocks of copper in Rotterdam not reported in the official statistics. A month later, the Netherlands Statistical Office admitted its data were flawed, because of a failure to distinguish between copper imported for domestic use and copper in transit.

Even assuming that statistics are correct, there can still be problems. For instance, car registration statistics are taken as a proxy for sales, but cars may be pre-registered by main dealers to meet year-end volume targets without there being equivalent sales to customers. Purchases of houses are 'stamped' by the UK Inland Revenue, thereby acting as a proxy for the level of activity in the housing market. However, the temporary increase in the stamp duty threshold to £250,000 in 1992 led to an artificial bunching of housing transactions in the third quarter of that year. In both cases, the statistics were correct but not representative of the underlying trend of consumer decision making.

The next class of statistics are *value figures* where, rather than counting the number of physical units, the monetary value is recorded. These tend to be used where the product is not homogeneous, literally enabling one to add apples and oranges; retail sales statistics would be one of the best examples. Obviously, the value measure is also used when dealing with monetary and banking statistics. Provisos are much the same as mentioned for the physical statistics. Over time, the impact of inflation reduces the usefulness of value series.

Finally (and for the reason mentioned above), we have the **pseudo-volume statistics**, which are value statistics adjusted for price changes in order to measure the underlying volume. This is done with, for example, engineering, capital investment and construction output. Here, the errors inherent in the initial data collection are compounded by errors in the estimation of price changes – a notoriously difficult area to measure accurately.

The 'warnings' above are given in the context of the use of published statistics as indicators of current trends. They apply equally to long term statistical series but here we have another measurement problem – ▷**long term changes in quality and performance relative to price.**◁ In its *Economic Focus*, *The Economist*[9] reviewed a paper by William Nordhaus of Yale University which argued that the change in the price of light had been overstated by 3.6% p.a. over a 200 year period. The improvements in the efficiency of sources of light were such that 'Conventional measures, even when prepared by careful statisticians who understand the problem, fail to capture these improvements'. It was suggested that the overstatement of price increases is common to a range of products – cars, computers, televisions, air conditioning, telephones, etc. Statistics that are expressed as monetary values and then deflated over time by price inflation which is overstated,[10] will understate volume growth. In addition, it will distort the relationship between that series and other series that are

---

9   22 October 1994.
10 The point is equally valid if it is price reductions which are understated.

more accurate, e.g. the relationship between any progressive technology product and gross domestic product (GDP).

One ought to refer also to *seasonally adjusted figures*, that wonderful concept that can mean I do not have a job all winter but, seasonally adjusted, I am working. There will be recognisable seasonal patterns to trade such as December retail toy sales, August car registrations in the UK but most seasonal variation is due to the weather. What the seasonal adjustment does is to remove the *average* deviation from the trend so that, other things being equal, each month or quarter will be the same; thus, in a normal year, the winter months will show the same value as the summer months. However, it is sometimes thought that all variation is adjusted, which is not the case. If there is a severe winter, leading to an unusually large fall in, say, construction output, the actual figures are only adjusted upwards by the normal seasonal variation. Strange though it may sound, it would still be correct to say that the seasonally adjusted winter construction figures had been adversely affected by severe weather.

One of the best ways to realise how statistics can change is to look at the impact of revisions to past data. When the construction output statistics were revised by the Department of Environment in 1993, to take fuller account of the output of small firms, it transpired that the most recent output figures needed to be increased by almost 20%. Nor was this a consistent increase, for the output of a decade earlier was left substantially unchanged. Graph 1.1 plots the ratio between the revised and the old statistics and shows how the long term trend had been distorted; however, the cyclical patterns were similar for both the old and the revised series.

Economics and accounting

No industrial or corporate forecast can hope to be accurate if the starting assumptions about the overall state of the economy are incorrect. There is, however, a wealth of literature on economic forecasting and there is no attempt to replicate it here; to use economists' terminology, it will be taken as given though, at a micro-economic level, there is overlap between the theory of the firm and sales forecasting.

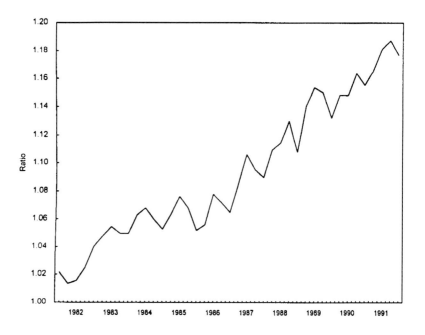

Graph 1.1 Revisions to construction output: ratio of revised versus old series (source: Department of the Environment).

A more difficult decision is the extent to which this book should discuss accounting issues for, like economics, there is a recognised body of material explaining accounting principles and, more relevant for the financial analyst, explaining how to detect whether a set of accounts actually reflects underlying realities. It is, of course, well recognised that the formal statement of profits can include huge subjectivities. Let us take a couple of examples, one showing the application of different international approaches and the other illustrating how prior years' accounts can be restated when profitability and cash flow subsequently deteriorate. As a prelude to listing its shares in New York, Daimler Benz published two versions of its 1993 interim figures – a profit of DM 168m under German accounting standards and a loss of DM 949m under US GAAP (generally accepted accounting principles). In the UK, Queen's Moat House produced its Annual Report for 1991 disclosing turnover of £543m and pre-tax profits of £90.4m; these were restated the following year as £315m turnover and a loss of £56.3m.

Many other examples could have been produced but for the most part, this book assumes that published profits are indeed 'true and fair', not because the author is naïve but because it is a necessary working assumption, from which one can deviate at a later point. The essence of the book is forecasting what is happening to the underlying business trends – not how one set of accountants chooses to portray them at any point in time. Nevertheless, later chapters discuss the interrelation between the forecasting of profits and their appropriate accounting definition, including the relationship between management accounts and published accounts, and 'profits smoothing'. We also look at the balance sheet as a source of information.

For those professionally employed in the broking houses and investing institutions, a crucial element in the profits forecasting exercise is the relationship between the forecaster and the management of the company whose profits are being forecast (or forecastee?). This relationship has changed radically over the past 30 years as both sides became closer, perhaps unhealthily so. The author's own memories of starting as an investment analyst in the early 1960s, in what was a research-based broker, is that contact with companies was no more than occasional and more often by telephone than in person. Neither was there the sector specialisation that is now the standard, with all its attendant detailed knowledge. (As a historical aside, stockbrokers seem to have moved from a position where one analyst covered several industries to several analysts covering one industry; the quantity of research has increased but a qualitative judgement might be harder to make.) More recently, the insider trading legislation has reduced, though scarcely eliminated, the flow of privileged information from the corporate sector to professional investors and that may lead to analysts returning more to their trade and less acting as retailers of the subject company's latest thoughts. Of course, being human, company representatives are usually happy to purvey good news but tend to be elusive in more difficult times (in itself, a useful profits indicator!). The realisation that the quality of the 'guidance' received during the recession was, in practice, less than helpful may do more to encourage independent clarity of thought than any amount of legislation and supervision.

2 Long term trends and the growth industry

Summary
Chapter 2 is concerned with long term industry growth but most particularly with the constraints to growth. It opens by discussing extrapolation, or the projection of past rates of growth, sometimes the only response of marketing and economics books to long term forecasting. The danger of indefinitely extrapolating historic trends is well known, as a result of which the approach is often dismissed as simplistic. However, this chapter offers an explanation of why, for much of the time, extrapolation can be a logical approach to forecasting.

Nevertheless, the prime concern of this chapter is not with the mathematics of projecting growth rates but with addressing the crucial question for the forecaster: when is the growth going to stop; and is there a framework we can use in a variety of differing circumstances? To do this, we use the concepts of product ownership (e.g. the number of washing machines owned) and of 'saturation' (i.e. the number of washing machines that might eventually be owned). We then show the relationship between the rate at which a given population is growing (typically forming an S-curve) and the annual sales derived therefrom. The key point is that it only needs a slow down in the rate of growth in ownership to cause an absolute fall in the annual sales of the product.

To provide examples for those who wish to see for themselves how a particular argument works, we need to construct tables covering time periods of up to 20 years; their size makes them look more daunting than they are. However, they are invariably accompanied by graphs to provide for easier illustration.

We discuss the simple relationships of one durable product to one household and explain how saturation level may be estimated. We then progress to the more complicated ownership patterns (more than one durable per household) and then to the impact of replacement demand. Product saturation and the S-curve are familiar concepts in many business books but discussions tend to be confined to consumer durables. However, although durables are by far the easiest of products to illustrate, they are but a small part of the economy. The latter part of the chapter extends the analysis to consumer non-durables, to capital goods, and to components and intermediates – areas rarely covered elsewhere.

Extrapolation of past trends: a justification

It used to be said in the stockbroking world that a long term investment was merely a short term decision that had gone wrong. However, there is a much clearer distinction between long term forecasting and short term forecasting techniques; the latter does not become the former through the mere passage of time. In long term forecasting the primary interest is in sustainable rates of growth over a period of years, with the concept of the growth company and, of particular interest to the forecaster, the growth company that goes ex-growth. Indeed, this is a point that must be stressed right at the beginning: ▷ **there are few prizes for forecasting that 5% growth is going to continue; the commercially valuable forecasts are those that identify the end of a growth trend.** ◁

It is the long term forecast that we are addressing in this chapter but to complete the contrast, the short term forecast is primarily concerned with economic and industrial cycles because, on a short time scale, the fluctuations in the cycle are significantly more important than the underlying growth rate. Cyclical forecasting and long term forecasting require separate techniques and, indeed, there are analysts who feel more at ease with one type of forecasting (and, hence, industry) than the other. Some industries tend to require one approach rather than the other. For instance, long term growth rates are of more concern in the electronics and pharmaceutical industries which are notable for the importance of new products, whereas the engineering and construction industries, which essentially involve products in the maturity phase of the product life cycle, are more receptive to cyclical analysis.

Why extrapolate?

Those business and economics books that cover forecasting frequently start (and finish) their explanation by discussing extrapolation, or the statistical projection of past trends into the future. According to the complexity desired, time series will use a variety of mathematical techniques designed to define the underlying historic trend and continue it. Statistical adjustments will remove any cyclical, seasonal or random elements from the series, leaving a trend line that as near as possible represents the historical growth rate. That growth rate can be projected either on a linear or curved form. Ample description of the methodology can be found in macro-economic or statistical textbooks.

Then follows the necessary explanation of why extrapolation has limitations as a forecasting tool; why the past may be no reliable guide to the future. Yet the question that is rarely asked is why *should* the past in any circumstances be assumed to offer a guide to the future. ▷**Why should the fact that demand for product A has** **grown by 5% a year for ten years be any guide to its growth in the 11th year?** ◁

As a first simple response, try to think what it means if there is no long term trend line, of some regular and quantifiable shape. The alternative must be an irregular progression, with the change between years arising on a random basis. Let us take the extreme case and imagine circumstances where demand for a product could move from zero to its maximum level in a year. The immediate introduction of identity cards might produce that effect for the fortunate supplier of the paperwork; or government regulations that a new safety product has to be installed in all cars within a year; high fashion; a new James Bond film; or any children's craze might be more readily observable examples.

Once we accept how unusual it is to find that full potential demand is reached within a period of a year, the easier it is to accept the normality of a gradual progression in the annual sales of a product as it moves from being, in the simplest of terms, little used to being widely used. But rather than merely accept it, much better to understand the underlying logic: three broad arguments can be produced in favour of a gradual progression in demand. Demand for new products is determined, other things being equal, by:

- consumers' awareness that those products exist and the consumers' wish to acquire them – *product familiarity*;
- consumers' ability to afford the purchase – *affordability*;
- the speed with which supply can be increased to satisfy demand – *supply constraints*.

Understanding the interplay of these motive forces helps the forecaster to understand why growth is taking place and to determine the extent to which that growth will continue.

Product familiarity

Leaving the influence of incomes to a later paragraph, demand in the early stages of a product's life cycle is determined by:

- awareness of a product's existence;
- increased familiarity with and exposure to the product; and
- 'keeping up with the Jones's' or whatever other psychological factor determines the uses to which we put our money.

It may be that a completely new product comes on the market, such as the video recorder or the mobile phone; or there may be a change in taste such as the switch from full cream milk to skimmed milk. Some people are quicker to react to new products than others, are more concerned with being up to date, or trying the latest ideas, all of which contributes to a gradual extension of ownership of the product. This progression is reinforced by changes in incomes and in the relative price of the product, discussed below.

There can also be a compulsory adoption of new products. Legislative changes also creative progressive movements in demand as government requirements are phased in over time. Thus, the introduction of smokeless zones in the 1960s and 1970s supported the rise in demand for smokeless fuel; and the introduction and subsequent tightening of minimum tread requirements for tyres led to increasing replacement demand for tyres.

Affordability

A product might be well recognised and desirable, but only affordable by a limited proportion of the population. As growth in consumer incomes spreads progressively through the population then, as disposable incomes rise, so an increasing proportion of the population will have the ability to purchase a given product. The extent to which demand increases as incomes increase (rather than in response to specific price changes) is known as the income elasticity of demand. This is a particularly long term influence on demand.

Price elasticity of demand, the extent to which demand responds to changes in the price of the product, can sometimes have a greater effect on widening the market. As output rises, increased economies of scale permit reductions in the relative price, thereby increasing the numbers who can afford to buy the product. The manufacturer may also have a pricing policy that seeks to maintain a high price in the early years, selling to that segment of the market prepared to pay high prices. This is followed by significant price reductions to widen the size of the market. These are features widely observable in the consumer electronics market but can be found in a variety of other industries – the hardback book followed by the paperback in publishing; automatic transmission, air-conditioning or any other new feature in the car industry.

Increased product familiarity tends to be the driving force in the early stages of growth, with price then income elasticity becoming more important in the mature growth phase. There are products that are predominately driven by awareness and acceptability and not price and income, e.g. the adoption of skimmed milk. For other products, it soon becomes a matter of price and income. Few households would choose not to have a car, or central heating, if financially affordable. An essential part of the forecaster's task is to understand which of these influences drives demand for the specific product.

18

Supply constraints

The early stages of growth produce significant annual percentage increases in demand and these can impose limitations on the producer's ability to supply. This is one reason why a change in government regulations requiring the use of a new product or the imposition of new standards (as instanced under 'Product familiarity' above) is deliberately phased in over a period of years to ensure that supply can cope, thereby creating its own inbuilt growth. Moreover, most companies are, to a greater or lesser degree, risk averse. Rapid growth in demand has to be anticipated in advance if it is to be supplied; the faster the rate of growth, the greater the capital commitment and, hence, the greater the risk.

An example of long term growth being driven by supply has been retailers such as Marks & Spencer and Sainsbury in the UK. Both have a recognised formula that is known to be affordable and popular. Yet if there is not a store in your locality, you cannot be a regular consumer of their product. As supply was increased each year by opening new stores in towns not previously served, so latent demand was able to translate into actual demand in one of the most controlled growth rates ever seen in commercial life. McDonalds provides a similar example across national boundaries.

Thus, if it is accepted that:

- product knowledge and aspirations only gradually permeate through a society;
- rising incomes and falling relative prices gradually permit a wider range of customers to afford the product; and
- suppliers might need to control the rate at which they increase production;

then the principle of a steady trend (be it linear or curved) in sales over time can be rationalised. ▷**Because the use of past growth rates as a predictive indicator is all too often criticised as simplistic, it is important to accept that for much of the time it is a perfectly acceptable approach, i.e. it works more often than not.**◁ The forecaster must understand why he is extrapolating; when it is legitimate; and when it might be leading him astray – read on.

The danger of extrapolating growth trends

When we talk about forecasting growth, we must clarify exactly what we think we are forecasting. Growth is not something that exists in its own right – it is a derived concept that is used by the statistician rather than by inhabitants of the real world. Individuals do not increase their expenditure on cars by 5%; they either buy a car or they do not. Collectively, a million people may buy a car in a given year, or buy one and a half million, or two million; this can be compared with previous years to calculate a growth rate but that is a derived calculation. Nevertheless, it is often easier to talk in terms of growth rates for products and companies; investors prefer faster-growing companies than slower-growing ones and it is the rate of growth that will be related to the return on the investment.

However, the danger in using rates of growth for forecasting purposes is that it is easy to lose touch with the physical reality of the underlying numbers. For instance, if a forecast contained the statement that, over a 25 year period, new car sales will grow at 10% p.a., does that immediately strike the reader as reasonable, or on the optimistic side, or as totally ridiculous? Talking about 10% growth for car sales may sound unrealistic to anyone who works with business data but the author has tried the question on graduate recruits who found nothing exceptionable about the statement. Yet the implication of that 10% growth rate is that at the end of the forecast period, every single household in the country would be buying a new car every year – and with no one left to buy the old car. Put the question in 'real' terms and there is little doubt what the answer would be: it is patently much easier to spot an unrealistic assumption about the future when it is expressed in absolute terms and related to the context. For those readers who would immediately have dismissed 10% growth as a working assumption and who think that I am putting up an 'Aunt Sally' for the sole purpose of knocking it, then try evaluating 5% growth as a working assumption, or 4%, or 3%. To test the validity of an assumed growth rate, at some point, it is necessary to translate that growth rate into real buying transactions.

 ▷ **So, the lesson must be, by all means think in terms of growth rates as a shorthand way of forecasting but do cross check what the outcome will look like in absolute terms. The faster the market is growing, the more important become the cross checks.** ◁

The forecaster's art is to know when it is appropriate to project past growth rates, in which case the forecast will undoubtedly be part of the general consensus, and when to shout 'Stop, I don't believe this is carrying on as it has done in the past; instead I predict a major change in trend'. This takes us back to the earlier warning on extrapolating and we can look at some of the reasons typically given for trend line extrapolation breaking down. The usual examples given are government action, war and acts of God. Unfortunately, although some types of external disturbances may be capable of prediction, they are irregular in occurrence and, by their nature, their timing is not easy to forecast.

However, the most important limitation to growth, and one that is frequently amenable to simple analysis and forecasting, is product saturation. ▷**The ability to recognise that saturation levels exist, even if they cannot be accurately measured, is crucial to the forecaster, whose successes will be identified with the occasions when he identifies a change in trend rather than predicts the continuation of existing trends.** ◁

Product ownership and saturation levels

If we accept that the limitation of extrapolation is that, like an errant child, it never knows when to stop, then the remainder of the chapter concentrates on how we can best determine the limits of growth. Textbooks on economics or on marketing frequently address long term forecasting via a discussion of the product life cycle, with its familiar stages of introduction, growth, maturity and decline, representing the differing profiles of annual sales of the product. Concepts such as saturation level or ownership of the product play a prominent role in the explanation of the product life cycle.

We are taking saturation level to be the maximum potential use of a product or service, 'use' representing a purchase transaction. 'Saturation level' indicates the upper limits to demand which could reasonably (the word is chosen deliberately) be expected for a given range of incomes. It is the comparison between the existing level of use and the eventual saturation level that indicates the capacity for future growth. ▷**However, it might as well be stated at the outset that there are problems in defining saturation in an**

21

intellectually rigorous manner. Nevertheless, one can use the concept sufficiently well to understand its effects and, on occasions, to quantify 'saturation level' accurately enough to draw important analytical conclusions. ◁

We now need to make an important distinction. Whereas the concept of saturation level can be applied to any product, be it durable or consumable, or to any service, ownership can only be applied to products that can be retained, i.e. durable goods. In this case, we are not directly interested in the maximum use of the product (how many times the vacuum cleaner is used) because that does not represent an economic transaction. Instead, we are interested in the maximum level of ownership (how many households own a vacuum cleaner) for it is the act of becoming an owner that creates the sale of the product.

▷ **For consumables, each upwards move towards saturation level represents an increase in demand,** ◁ e.g. the higher the proportion of people using paper kitchen towels, the higher will be the annual demand. ▷ **For durables, each upwards move in ownership levels does not necessarily mean an increase in new sales – the level of sales for durables depends not on the absolute level of ownership but on the rate of increase in ownership,** ◁ e.g. an increase in the level of ownership of cars normally means an increase in the annual demand for car servicing, for petrol, for tax discs. However, an increase in the level of ownership of cars does not necessarily mean an increase in the annual demand for cars. It is the relationship between ownership and annual demand that we are to explain in the next section.

Consumer durables

We begin with consumer durables, where the numerical analysis of ownership is most straightforward. Product ownership as a concept is readily understandable for large, infrequently purchased durables[11] such as washing machines and cars, but it can also be extended to a wide range of frequently purchased and low price durables – compact discs are taken as an example later. We show how the path towards product saturation is of a

---

11 Sometimes called 'big ticket' items.

recognisable pattern, typically an 'S' curve; it is the changing slope of this curve that determines the quite different patterns of new or incremental sales that is encompassed within the description of the product life cycle.

The one-to-one relationship

The simplest ownership profiles are those where physical dictates suggest one object per person, or per adult or per household. The best example is housing where the population (or numerical stock) of houses roughly equals the number of households – a relationship that has existed throughout the twentieth century (Table 2.1).

There are households that do not have a housing unit of their own but the personal motivation and social pressures are such that this is a very small percentage. There are households that occupy more than one house but this group, too, represents a very small percentage of the total. The marginal benefit from the ownership of the second dwelling is so small compared with the benefit from the first and the additional discretionary income needed is so large

Table 2.1 Households and dwellings: England and Wales[12]

Census date	Total dwellings (000)	Households (000)	Dwellings/households
1911	7 691	7 943	0.97
1921	7 979	8 739	0.91
1931	9 400	10 233	0.92
1941	11 400	11 300	1.01
1951	12 530	13 259	0.95
1961	14 646	14 724	1.00
1971	17 024	16 876	1.01
1981	18 995	18 334	1.04
1991	20 748	20 131	1.03

Source: *Housing Policy, DoE, 1977, Housing and Construction Statistics (annual).*

12 Note: Since 1911 there have been changes of definition of both households and dwellings in the UK; further background is given in *Housing Policy* DoE, 1977, Part 1, pp. 14–15 and *Household Projections England 1989–2011.* For instance, under the 1971 Census definitions, people with a room of their own and catering separately, but sharing a sitting room, were counted as separate households; under the 1981 Census definitions, they were counted as one household.

that second ownership will stay a small percentage of the total for most forecasters' foreseeable horizons.

The one-to-one relationship is important because it represents a natural benchmark against which ownership levels can be judged. Thus we can also understand the logic behind one household, one vacuum cleaner, where ownership is 95% and 'saturation' clearly exists. Near saturation levels also exist for washing machines, freezers and telephone lines. At the other end of the scale are dishwashers (16%) then, further down, the home facsimile machine or, yet to come, the video phone – all of which would typically be one per household unit. These are products which we may assume have the capability of achieving a one-to-one relationship (or 100% ownership, or saturation level, or whatever expression you feel comfortable with) and can therefore make assumptions about the future based on a numerically rational framework.

The one-to-one relationships can be fine tuned from the general to the particular as product saturation can be defined for specific segments of the population, determined by age, sex, accommodation, occupation, hobbies and so on. Thus, estimates of saturation level for do-it-yourself (DIY) products would be based on the population of owner occupier households rather than all households; estimates for computer chess sets would be more useful if made by reference to the number of chess players.

Ownership levels and the S-curve

In Table 2.2 we show a theoretical ownership profile. For ease of calculation, our assumptions are that saturation level will be one million units, reached 20 years after the introduction of the product. If the progression to saturation level is a straight line then this would equate to an average annual demand of 50 000 units before stopping abruptly (though replacement demand would prevent this). In practice, ownership levels do not increase in a straight line. After the initial introductory phase, there is rapid adoption of a product in the early stages of its development, while the last few years will be see the slow conversion of the remaining non-users. Thus, the move towards saturation point is likely to be curved, typically S-shaped, clearly illustrated in Graph 2.1.

Table 2.2 Theoretical ownership profile (see Graph 2.1)

Year	1	2	3	4	5	6	7	8	9	10
% ownership	0.5	1.5	4	8	15	25	35	44	52	59
Units owned (000)	5	15	40	80	150	250	350	440	520	590

Year	11	12	13	14	15	16	17	18	19	20
% ownership	66	72	78	83	87	91	94	96	98	100
Units owned (000)	660	720	780	830	870	910	940	960	980	1000

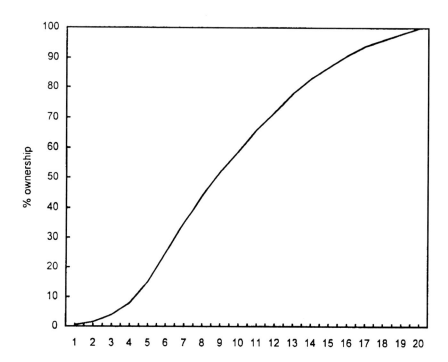

Graph 2.1 Theoretical ownership profile (Table 2.2).

Ownership and new sales

We have already said that ▷ **the speed at which the ownership of a durable product moves towards saturation level determines the**

25

annual increment of demand. ◁ In Table 2.3, we have derived annual sales figures from the ownership profile given in Table 2.2. Each year's new sales equal the difference between the number of units owned in any two periods. We can now clearly see the impact that a slowing down in the rate of increase in ownership levels has on net annual sales. Year 7 demonstrates the point clearly: ownership rises from 25% to 35% but as there had also been a 10 point increase in ownership levels the year before, the increase in new sales remains level at 100 000 units. In year 8, where there is still a substantial increase in ownership (35% to 44%), it is not quite as large a jump as in year 7, and the level of new sales falls 10%. That reduction in new sales continues all the while that market penetration is increasing. In graphical form, this would appear as in Graph 2.2, where the ownership level is contrasted with the change in new sales; in effect, the latter is plotting the rate of change in the former.

Observation of the figures in the table and some elementary mathematics leads to simple conclusions. We can see that ownership is *not* the same as annual sales. New sales are a function of the *change* in levels of ownership. To illustrate the terminology with a common example, the total number of cars owned in the UK (referred to as the car population, the stock or the car pool) totals some 24 million; the rate at which that car pool increases, say half

Table 2.3 Ownership and new sales

Year	1	2	3	4	5	6	7	8	9	10
No. of units owned (000)	5	15	40	80	150	250	350	440	520	590
Change, i.e. new sales	5	10	25	40	70	100	100	90	80	70
% change		100	150	60	75	43	0	−10	−11	−13

Year	11	12	13	14	15	16	17	18	19	20
No. of units owned (000)	660	720	780	830	870	910	940	960	980	1000
Change, i.e. new sales	70	60	60	50	40	40	30	20	20	20
% change	0	−14	0	−17	−20	0	−25	−33	0	0

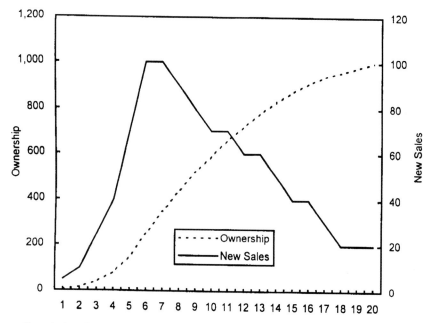

Graph 2.2 Ownership versus new sales.

a million a year, is the *net* annual demand.[13] Indeed, the reader might be excused for regarding those comments as exceedingly obvious, no more than basic common sense. That is as may be, but the author has seen major companies make fundamental errors in forecasting their own product demand by ignoring the mathematics of the move to saturation level.

At the risk of over-emphasising the point, ▷ **one of the basic errors made by forecasters is to concentrate on rising ownership of a durable product, ignoring the fact that new sales are a function of the rate of change in the ownership of that product.** ◁

---

13 The problem with examples drawn from the real world is that they never fit simply the point to be demonstrated and, in our car example, the complicating factor is that some of the annual demand comes not from an increase in the total size of the car pool, but from a replacement of old stock, hence the use of the word net. Nevertheless, the concept of the relationship between the total product population and its annual increase, or new demand, is straightforward.

Going Ex-Growth

Here we come to the whole object of the exercise. The point at which annual sales can go 'ex-growth' is suprisingly early in the ownership curve. The fastest rate of percentage increase in demand will be seen at the lower levels of product ownership but, once these have been passed, it becomes very difficult to sustain fast rates of growth. If, for instance, 15% ownership level has been reached then 30% annual growth in new sales can only be sustained for seven years before full saturation level is reached; 20% growth could last for ten years. Once the ownership level reaches 30%, a point that observers might consider left plenty of potential, the limits on growth are that much tighter – 30% growth could only continue for six years before reaching 100% ownership and this makes no allowance for the inevitable tailing off in growth as the 100% level is approached.

 When a product has achieved a modest level of market penetration, fast rates of growth in ownership can be sustained for only a limited period of time – and, as we have seen from the tables above, those periods of time can be quantified. Thus, if we know the historical ownership profile, together with an estimate of the saturation level, we can construct an S-curve. If we have an S-curve we can calculate annual sales; and if we can calculate annual sales then we can see when growth in annual sales is likely to stop.

A real example taken from the *Financial Times* in September 1994 shows the way in which statistics can give the wrong impressions of growth if they are not worked through. The article 'Hearing an explosion on the grapevine' discussed the rapid rate of growth in ownership of mobile phones and included figures as per Table 2.4. The article went on to say that a US consultancy 'estimates that the total will reach 20m by the end of this year [1994]. They and other analysts believe that the 25% growth rate could accelerate into 1995 and 1996.' The picture presented was of unallayed growth, yet if we look at the figures in the way in which we suggested earlier, and put in the estimate for 1994 (Table 2.5), then a more

Table 2.4 US mobile communications market							
Year	1987	1988	1989	1990	1991	1992	1993
No. of subscribers (m)	1.2	2.1	3.5	5.3	7.6	11.0	16.0

Source: *Cellular Telecommunications Industry Association.*

Table 2.5 US mobile communications market – a further look

Year	1987	1988	1989	1990	1991	1992	1993	1994 Est.
No. of subscribers (m)	1.2	2.1	3.5	5.3	7.6	11.0	16.0	20.0
% change		75	67	51	43	45	45	25
New sales (m)		0.9	1.4	1.8	2.3	3.4	5.0	4.0
% change			56	29	28	48	47	−25

complex picture emerges, and one that highlights the difference between

- the growth in a consumable product or service (the number of subscribers and therefore the number of people making telephone calls);
- the ownership of the durable (the mobile phone) where a decline in the rate of growth means a fall in the number of new telephones sold.

Nowhere in the article does it say that the growth in mobile telephone ownership, though large in absolute numbers, is actually slowing down and that the projected ownership figure for 1994 implies a fall of a quarter in new sales of telephones. Even if the ownership figure turned out to be 21 million, it implies no growth in new sales. And what is the 25% growth that analysts believe could accelerate in 1995 and 1996?[14] An exercise for the reader is to take the number of households in the US, or the number of full time employed people, assume (or make an intelligent guess if you prefer) a level of ownership in the year 2000 and see what limits this places on the total number of subscribers and, hence, growth in new sales of mobile telephones.

> One hundred per cent ownership is not usually achieved
> – or how to determine saturation level

We should now be clear that if we are forecasting new sales for a consumer durable (remember we are still ignoring replacement

14 The fact that the estimates eventually proved conservative does not alter the basic point that it is all too easy to draw incorrect conclusions about annual sales from rising ownership statistics.

sales), we need to set out the simple mathematical relationship between ownership and new sales. However, ▷**a basic error when looking at ownership statistics is to equate saturation level with the maximum number of people or households for whom that product could theoretically be applicable, rather than for the much smaller number of people who actually have a requirement for the product.**◁ The reason for this, of course, lies in one of the opening comments, namely that forecasters feel easiest when working with published statistics. It is easier to obtain the data for large population groups in the UK using the *National Population Projections* or the *Projections of Households* – all adults between 25 and 60, or all females over 20, or even all households in Cambridge – but it is far more difficult to obtain the number of people who would be genuinely interested in acquiring the product. We give an example of this particular mistake in Chapter 7.

So far, we have looked at ownership on the basis of a natural one-to-one relationship within the total population or relevant segment of the population. We have assumed that the only barrier to achieving full ownership is income and general awareness of the existence of the product. There are, of course, products that not everybody wants whatever the price – a wheelchair, a fortnight in a holiday camp, a home knitting machine, opera tickets or a hot air balloon trip. In its effects, this is not far removed from products that would not be wanted unless the price was so much cheaper that it is not a relevant issue; or the same effect is achieved by the individual's income being several times higher. A Rolls or Ferrari might be examples, or even one's own helicopter.

How, therefore, might one postulate what that effective maximum ownership level might be? One could define the potential market so tightly that it automatically defined maximum potential ownership. This is what market research surveys try to achieve using interviews and sampling techniques to ascertain how many people have a potential interest in, to draw from the examples above, visiting the opera or a holiday camp. This is an expensive and time consuming exercise and therefore only available as an option with the support of a corporate budget. It is preparatory research normally undertaken by companies as a prelude to their own corporate activities (i.e. not for forecasting the activity of third parties) or by market research firms hoping to sell the results across the relevant industry (at high prices). These surveys may be available in libraries, or summarised in the Press.[15] If they are not available, or have never been done, then what options are open to the forecaster?

The common approach is to take the closest available statistical grouping and assume (we will discuss how) a maximum potential ownership, be it 20%, 40% or 75%. This is the approach typically seen with high price consumer durables where the ownership percentage is related to the total number of households in existence, irrespective of the fact that many families may have no desire whatsoever to own, for instance, a video recorder. The assumption of a percentage below 100% is a shorthand way of allowing for the fact that some part of that population would not have been included had there been a more effective way to define the population group. In trying to estimate (guess?) a realistic medium term ownership level, how do you pluck an appropriate percentage out of the air? It is always satisfying to have a neat statistical answer to such questions but the obvious first response has to be by using common sense, observation and experience.

▷ **The fact that one cannot plot common sense on a graph makes it no less valuable an approach in assessing how the human race may respond to a given set of opportunities.** ◁   ⋈

There are, of course, ways in which one might supplement common sense and one of the possibilities open to those forecasting in the UK is to look at what has already happened in more affluent communities, i.e. those who have moved further up the graph of income elasticity. Thus, if dishwasher ownership is 45%[16] in the US against only 16%[17] in the UK then at least there is an alternative scenario that might act as a model for the UK. Unfortunately, national characteristics are not uniform and one would have to be careful about extrapolating domestic air conditioning statistics from the US, triple glazing from Sweden or Paris Disneyland from Florida. If those caveats seem obvious, the author has seen attempts to use more than one of those comparisons.

Without looking internationally, comparisons can also be made with apparently similar products that are at a later stage in their life cycle. Thus, the introduction of any new consumer durable will be accompanied by attempts to identify previous products with

15 See Chapter 5 on Sources of information.
16 *Statistical Abstract of the United States 1994*; ownership in 1990.
17 1993.

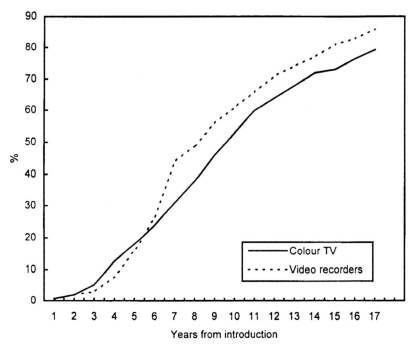

Graph 2.3 Ownership profiles: colour TV and video recorders (source: British Radio & Electronic Equipment Manufacturers' Association).

equivalent characteristics, price and customer appeal. As can be seen in Graph 2.3, the video recorder, for example, had an almost identical ownership profile to colour televisions.[18]

To recap, we have demonstrated the link between ownership and new sales; emphasised the need to prepare a matrix so that the relationship can more accurately be assessed; and explored how we might determine saturation level. With this framework in mind, we are going to show what happens when we move away from the simple one-to-one ownership–product relationship and then make the whole thing more realistic by introducing replacement demand.

Multiple purchases, or how many radios in your house?

There has been an implicit assumption that saturation level for a durable product could not be higher than the relevant population

18 Year 1 was deemed to be the first year in which ownership reached $\frac{1}{2}$%.

from which the purchasers are naturally drawn – one-to-one is a limit. However, many products that used to have a one-to-one relationship have subsequently moved to multiple purchasing. The author was brought up after World War II, like most of that generation, with a single radio (or wireless) in the family house. The concept of having additional radios for different rooms, or radios owned separately by individual children, did not arise. For illustration, I counted the number of radios now in my household's possession and, throwing in the car radios and radio alarms, the total reached double figures. The factors permitting the development of multiple purchasing are well understood, and touched on earlier – a substantial reduction in the relative price level, higher discretionary incomes particularly among the young and, perhaps more than anything, a change in technology that made the product portable. And all this happened at the same time as the introduction of television, a competing and ostensibly more attractive medium.

The decline in relative price plays an important role in increasing the level of ownership. As already indicated, this may happen over time as a result of progressive economies of scale and consequent cost reductions. The phasing of the price reductions may also be a deliberate management strategy designed to obtain high margins from a small (typically the high income segment) proportion of the market for a period of time, before targeting the mass market. Examples can be found in computers and proprietary drugs.

What forecasting conclusions are there to be drawn? Primarily, it is that once the one-to-one relationship has been left well behind, the forecasting techniques discussed above have less relevance and should be recognised as such. The 'radio' product has become a discretionary consumer durable where the stimulus to purchase is determined more by casual whim, minor convenience (wouldn't it be handy to have a separate radio in the bathroom?) and the general level of consumer affluence, than by the very strong desire to have the first radio in a household. The approach taken in assessing this generalised level of demand will be discussed later but for the time being we want to use the radio as an example in pattern recognition. Because improving technology and rising real incomes permits the development of multiple ownership, it does not follow that it necessarily creates it. Is it possible, therefore, to distinguish between those products that have the potential to become 'radios' and those that we might typify as 'toasters'?

Like the radio, the toaster is also a product of modern technology where the price is so low that for most families it is not a major consideration. Yet, and for reasons that hardly need spelling out, toaster ownership still largely conforms to the one product, one household relationship. We have been spared a multiplicity of toasters in every room, following us in the car and on the train and compounded by teenage children toasting in their bedrooms.

In forecasting demand for consumer durables which have reached or are approaching 100% ownership on a one-to-one basis, the crucial question then becomes: am I forecasting for a radio, i.e. will the size of its population continue to expand if relative prices and incomes are supportive; or am I forecasting for a toaster, i.e. is it a product that has reached a natural physical maturity. 'Radio' examples include television, where multiple ownership is becoming more frequent, or telephone extensions. In a different way, the watch, which a generation ago followed the classic one adult, one product relationship has extended its population of owners to children and broadened it to multiple ownership as watches became a fashion product. In contrast, the toaster example can be paralleled in vacuum cleaners, dishwashers, burglar alarms. The distinguishing characteristic of the toaster as against the radio is the complete lack of relevance for a duplicate product; indeed, there is sometimes a positive disadvantage in that space has to be found for it.

There are interesting in-between examples of limited multiple purchasing of which cars are the most important. For decades, the forecasting relationship was determined by the steady progression towards one household, one car. Then, during the 1960s and 1970s, changes in social mobility and rising living standards saw the emergence of the two car family, followed later by the three car family as teenage children became owners. Interestingly, households with only one car reached a plateau in 1970 (Graph 2.4) while two car households continued to expand.

However, this increase in ownership is not a latent 'radio' example waiting only for higher living standards to push car ownership yet higher. Cars have ownership disadvantages including a high annual ownership cost over and above the original purchase cost, and space or storage disadvantages. It can be understood that the benefits of car ownership will override these costs so that there is a progressive move through one family,

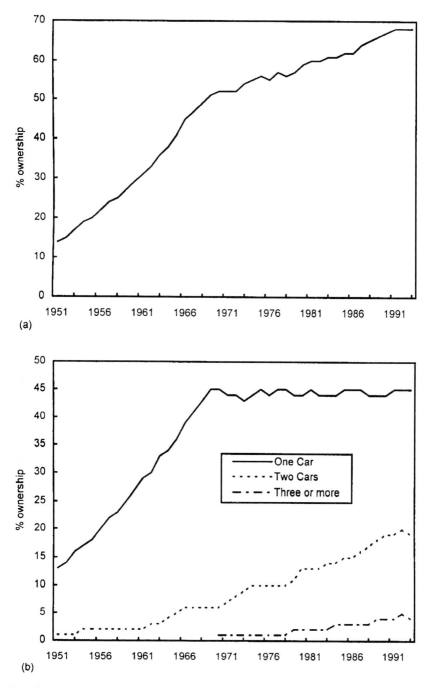

Graph 2.4 Car ownership: (a) % of households owning a car; (b) by number of cars (source: General Household Survey).

one car to one adult, one car. However, the marginal benefit to one individual of having a second car appears so small in relation to the additional costs (space, insurance) that a limit to the potential saturation level can be postulated.

To summarise the stages involved in the durable forecasting process:

- Define the relevant population – all householders, children, footballers, etc.
- Estimate a percentage ownership and terminal year, e.g. 60% within 15 years.
- Use an S-curve to estimate the ownership figures year by year.
- From the annual ownership figures, calculate the annual change, i.e. new sales of the product.
- When approaching high saturation levels, assess whether the product is suitable for multiple purchasing.

Replacement demand

So far, we have been discussing the demand for consumer durable products as if they lasted for ever. Regrettably that is not the case and the replacement of items previously purchased represents an important part of total demand. Establishing the proportion of total demand that is provided by the first, or original, sale and by subsequent replacement sales is crucial to the forecast, for the replacement element will provide a continuing level of demand even when 100% ownership has been achieved. Different levels of replacement demand can be observed.

- Replacement demand will be higher in relation to original equipment for short life products (an office worker's suit) than for a long life product (a house).
- Replacement demand will be low in the early stages of a product's maturity cycle, i.e. when ownership is low and original equipment demand is growing rapidly, e.g. home fax machines.
- Conversely, replacement demand will be high when the product has reached saturation level, e.g. vacuum cleaners.

In other words, replacement is a function of ownership and product life.

A distinction must be drawn between two types of what we loosely term replacement demand:

- The genuine replacement demand that has arisen because the product is no longer fulfilling its original function – it is either beyond repair or of an appearance that is no longer compatible with its original purpose.
- Replacement demand where the new generation of product is so technologically superior that it renders the earlier product obsolescent in the view of the user, though it still adequately fulfils its original purpose.

Obsolescence can often be regarded as much the creation of a new product in its own right as necessary replacement; the product has changed to the point where it can be regarded as substantially different in nature. Thus, perfectly good black and white televisions were jettisoned in favour of colour. A more recent example is that of personal computers that continued to fulfil the function for which they were originally purchased being replaced by computers with faster operating speeds and bigger memories. Sometimes the owner has little option but to accept that his product has become technologically obsolescent because it is no longer being supported. To continue with the computer example, new operating programs may require larger memory. Music lovers with expensive record players may have been 'forced' to purchase a compact disc player because new classical releases are only in CD form and no longer issued as long playing records.

Where genuine replacement demand ceases and technological replacement begins is unclear, for the extent to which owners are prepared to tolerate increasingly aged products will depend upon the extent to which the replacement will give enhanced performance or satisfaction. Again, it is helpful to recognise the patterns represented by the extremes. Examples of products that are only replaced when they break down might be central heating boilers or light bulbs; products that are replaced while still fully serviceable include our earlier computer example, fashion electronics and, indeed, the whole world of fashion clothing which appears to be structured on the principle that, once seen, it can never be used again.

If we return to the 20 year run of data shown for ownership and new sales, as shown in Tables 2.2 and 2.3, we can overlay an assumed replacement rate. Table 2.6 (illustrated in Graph 2.5) takes a replacement life of five years and, of course, those initial replacement sales in years 6–10 will themselves need replacing and so on; in each five year period, the replacement rate rises as a percentage of the total population and replacement sales account for an increasing proportion of total sales. What would have become a period of relentless decline in new sales is replaced by a period of slow growth with the occasional year of decline. There are also mini-peaks in year 11, five years after the peak level of initial equipment sales and then again in year 16, a further five years on. This is a somewhat artificial example but products that have been introduced over a relatively rapid period can, indeed, produce such replacement booms. Any variety of tables could have been produced with different patterns of new sales and different replacement rates. To repeat the comment above, for the forecaster, it is essential to establish the broad nature of the replacement pattern before determining the probable pattern of future sales.

We finish this section with an example drawn from the real world. Graph 2.6 shows the growth in ownership of video recorders and the annual sales. The early years of ownership are accompanied by rapid growth in annual sales, but as ownership approaches 30% we see the fall in new sales occurring. Thereafter, the impact of replacement sales is felt and we can even see the minor peaks that we managed to produce in our theoretical Graph 2.5.

Consumer non-durables

Saturation level for consumables

The concept of different levels of ownership, is easily recognisable for durable products, however complicated it may be in practice to quantify. When addressing consumables[19] one has to recognise

---

19 The usual statistical term is consumer non-durable, as in the heading, but it is never wholly satisfactory to define something in terms of what it is not; 'consumables' clearly indicates the nature of the products we are discussing.

Table 2.6 Illustration of replacement demand

Year	1	2	3	4	5	6	7	8	9	10	11	12	13	14	15	16	17	18	19	20
% ownership	0.5	1.5	4	8	15	25	35	44	52	59	66	72	78	83	87	91	94	96	98	100
Units owned (000)	5	15	40	80	150	250	350	440	520	590	660	720	780	830	870	910	940	960	980	1000
Change, i.e. new sales	**5**	**10**	**25**	**40**	**70**	**100**	**100**	**90**	**80**	**70**	**70**	**60**	**60**	**50**	**40**	**40**	**30**	**20**	**20**	**20**
% change		100	150	60	75	43	0	-10	-11	-13	0	-14	0	-17	-20	0	-25	-33	0	0
Replacement sales						5	10	25	40	70	100	100	90	80	70	70	60	60	50	40
											5	10	25	40	70	100	100	90	80	70
																5	10	25	40	70
Total replacement						**5**	**10**	**25**	**40**	**70**	**105**	**110**	**115**	**120**	**140**	**175**	**170**	**175**	**170**	**180**
Total sales	**5**	**10**	**25**	**40**	**70**	**105**	**110**	**115**	**120**	**140**	**175**	**170**	**175**	**170**	**180**	**215**	**200**	**195**	**190**	**200**
% change			150	60	75	50	5	5	4	17	25	-3	3	-3	6	19	-7	-3	-3	5
Replacement rate (%)						2.0	2.9	5.7	7.7	11.9	15.9	15.3	14.7	14.5	16.1	19.2	18.1	18.2	17.3	18.0

39

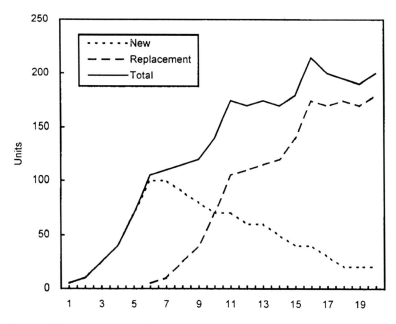

Graph 2.5 Impact of replacement demand.

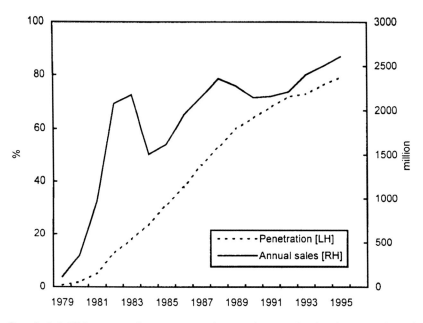

Graph 2.6 Video recorders – ownership and annual sales (source: British Radio & Electronic Equipment Manufacturers' Association).

first that there is a definitional problem in that durables merge into consumables: durables tend to be regarded as both long lasting and high cost, whereas consumables are seen as both short life and low cost. The distinction is recognisable though not always strictly logical. My address book, for instance, has probably had a longer life than my personal computer.

Can the concept of saturation levels be used in consumable products? One economics textbook stated 'Clearly for non-durable products ... there is no reason why saturation should ever be reached.' It seems equally clear to me that saturation level can be reached for the individual consumer and, if so, then for a pool of consumers – if in doubt, start eating the Mars bars now. The more relevant question appears to be, can saturation level be quantified with sufficient accuracy to be a useful analytical tool?

The short answer is sometimes and only with care. One can accept the principle that: 'It seems likely that there is a point past which, whatever is done, no more sales will be achieved.'[20] The concept of maximum use is easily developed. For instance, if one is looking at restaurant dinners then multiplying the population by 365 puts a maximum on potential demand, but that calculation is so far removed from the foreseeable reality that it is of little practical help. Other products defy even that exercise in theoretical limitation. What is the maximum number of books or records that could be purchased? For this type of product we are much more likely to be using income and price elasticities, recognising that sales are linked to relative pricing and consumer incomes. But before then, there are still a number of useful approaches that the forecaster can adopt.

Beware the false consumable

One thing that we should do first when looking at so-called consumables is to remind ourselves that some of them are really durables in disguise (we take compact discs as an example below). They are products that are bought so frequently, and at a sufficiently low price, that they are regarded as consumables; however, they have all the characteristics of ownership, and the

20 Saunders, J A, Sharp, J A and Will, S F, *Practical Business Forecasting*, 1987.

statistical analysis we applied in discussing durables remains relevant. This point could have been made, perhaps more logically, in the durables section but it has been left here for a psychological reason – to emphasise how important it is to realise that products that, by their price and frequency of purchase, might present themselves as consumables are really durables. ▷**Recognise the false consumable for what it is and the thought process is off to a flying start.** ◁

There is also a difference of degree between the 'false consumable' and what are often termed the 'big ticket' durables that we were taking as examples previously. The frequency of purchase is so far removed from the one-to-one relationship that there looks to be a total inability to quantify the ownership numbers – so why bother? However, it may still be possible to identify the concept of ownership and to quantify the saturation effect. If we pick up on one of the examples used in the discussion on obsolescence – compact disc players – we can look at the implication for the discs themselves.

We have already argued, a few paragraphs earlier, that there was no practical way of quantifying the maximum potential number of books or records that might be purchased. But that does not prevent us from thinking about the pattern of such purchases. The introduction of CD players meant the rebuilding of personal record libraries. Confining ourselves just to classical music, there is a recognised catalogue of work that, tenors apart, tends not to change much over time. It is reasonable, therefore, to suppose that the purchase of a player will be followed by a high rate of purchases of discs to play on the machine. There will come a point for most individuals when they have built, or rebuilt, their library of discs to the desired level and further purchases will drop back to an occasional level. It would be expected that these disc-purchasing patterns would follow behind the sale of players like a wave and the logic of the buying pattern that we have outlined above suggests, therefore, an eventual downturn in the sale of classical compact discs. It may not be easy to apply numbers to this example, nor to predict the turning point with any degree of confidence. However, an understanding of the saturation concept inherent in classical disc purchases should at the very least be alerting the forecaster to the probability of a downturn.

Graph 2.7 shows the rise in CD penetration to 56% of all households by 1994, coupled with the rise in annual sales of

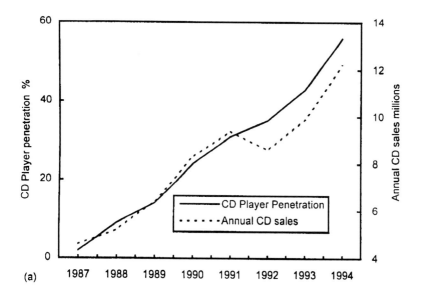

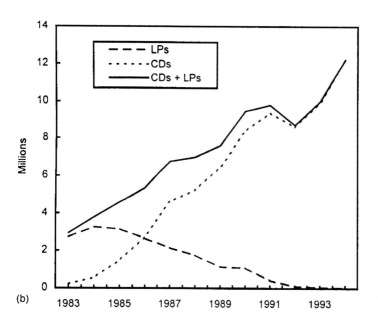

Graph 2.7 Classical compact discs: (a) CD players and classical CD discs;
(b) classical records (source: BPI Statistical Handbook).

classical CDs; Graph 2.7(b) shows that substitution of CDs for vinyl long playing records was almost total by the early 1990s. These two factors should have been sending warning signals: the high penetration of CD players (and, hence, peak CD buying patterns) and the elimination of the competing long playing records (nothing left to attack).

A few months after drafting the above paragraph, the *Daily Telegraph*[21] carried an article headed 'Record Industry In A Spin: The biggest names in music are getting a rude shock as labels react ruthlessly to a glut in the market for classical CDs'. The article suggested that 'The causes of crisis go back to two decades or more, but the present catastrophe can be traced primarily to a collapse of podium authority.' Nowhere in the article was there a recognition of the concept of product saturation, nor its mathematical inevitability, nor the improbability that demand could be coaxed back up to its earlier levels.

And now for the genuine consumable

We have already recognised that the quantification of growth or, to be more accurate, the limits on growth is easier with infrequently purchased, high value durables with a definable ownership profile. The further we move away from that, the more difficult becomes the task of quantifying maximum demand. Consumables represent the other end of the spectrum and we started by minimising the problem, trying to show how many consumables really have the characteristics of durables. The compact disc example can be widely applied – the market for men's suits or squash racquets, etc. But even where the product is a genuine consumable, there is often scope for detailed numerical analysis based on the principle of saturation.

An excellent example can be found in the pharmaceutical industry where it is rare (though not unknown) to consume the cure if not suffering from the relevant ailment. It is possible to quantify the number of sufferers from a particular ailment and then to distinguish between those drugs that alleviate or temporarily cure the symptoms (an antibiotic taken for ten days); a continuous treatment (such as a daily anti-arthritic drug); and

21 22 April 1996.

those that help eradicate or prevent disease (a vaccine). Three entirely different demand profiles can then be constructed.

Forecasters will frequently be faced with products and services for which there are no obvious statistics or at least nothing that is readily in the public domain. A common scenario is a company announcing that it has a new product; the press release also conveniently tells the reader that the company has estimated the size of the market to be two million, or 50 000 a week, or whatever. It expects to gain 20% of this estimated market and, hey presto, you have a sales forecast. But what to do with it, or how to check it? Is there any alternative but to accept it as authoritative? What may surprise people is that, once they learn how to think quantitatively, they can often estimate the broad magnitude of a market without even rising from their chair. That is not to say that they can produce accurate figures but, and this is the important point, they can produce a range within which they expect the answer to fall. That is how the forecaster begins to assess and to question the statements that companies make.

Let us take a mundane example and think how we might determine saturation level for a consumer service such as men's haircuts, a market that is already saturated but provides a good working example. Try pausing for a moment and do the calculation on the back of the proverbial envelope. Hopefully, you have a rough idea of the total population (if you do not, you are probably reading the wrong book). From there, you have a simple calculation for the male population. Guess the proportion that goes to a commercial hairdresser and how many times a year they go and you have the annual number of haircuts. Perhaps later you can fine tune your answer by looking at the actual population statistics and giving a little more thought to the proportions of the population that never visit a hairdresser but the original answer is likely to be of the right order of magnitude. Divide by 300 working days and you have the average number of haircuts per day. You will not be out by a factor of ten. You will very quickly be able to make a judgement on the size of the market and, most important, make a judgement on whether a forecast that is presented to you makes sense. (Just to emphasise points already made, you need to distinguish between products that are used with every haircut, and the stock of equipment that is used by every hairdresser.) Another *a priori* example is taken in the capital goods section below.

The fact that it is impossible to determine the saturation level for a product does not mean that the concept is invalid nor that judgements on the position in the ownership curve cannot be approximated – as we did with the compact disc example above. Significantly above average rates of growth will eventually decline as the (unquantifiable) saturation level is approached. It is optimistic to pretend that the timing of the decline in the rate of growth can necessarily be predicted but if the forecaster has the S-shaped curve constantly in mind, he is more likely to be able to recognise the signs.

Income elasticity

The determination of saturation level is important because it enables us to quantify the limits to growth and estimate the way in which those limits may be reached. However, it remains the case that for many products it is not easy to estimate saturation levels. Whereas there would probably be a broad measure of agreement between forecasters on the total market for haircuts (try it with your colleagues) there would be no consensus on restaurant meals – try that out as well and the estimates here could differ by a factor of ten! Fortunately, for this type of product, the rate of long term change is relatively gradual and correlated more with changes in the level of consumer income. Moreover, in the real world, few companies are predominantly dependent on one product or even a narrow range of products; they may serve broad markets such as packaged foods, cosmetics, home decorating or motor components. Even worse, they may be supplying an international market (in reality, a series of domestic markets) with complications that we will touch on in Part II ('Disparate businesses' in Chapter 6).

For those products where the rate of change is not determined by any readily forecastable saturation level, or where the product spread is too large to permit such analysis, a measure of the extent to which demand varies with income will be required. Economists use the concept of income elasticity of demand (IED) which is the ratio between the increase in demand and the increase in income. Thus, if a 1% increase in income produces a 2% growth in demand, there is an IED of 2; if demand grows by less than incomes, say a half per cent, there is an IED of 0.5; and if demand actually falls (a so-called 'inferior good') then the IED is negative.

Up-to-date estimates of income elasticities are not widely available (though without ever making these calculations, most laymen, let alone professional forecasters, could compile a rough league table of relative growth). One set of income elasticities was that provided for the food industry in 1989;[22] these showed no identified product with an elasticity greater than unity (fruit juice was the highest with 0.94) while many of the traditional staples had negative elasticities, i.e. the quantity of demand was actually lower in the higher income ranges (margarine –0.44, sugar –0.54 and potatoes –0.48). Estimates of income elasticity such as in the UK Food Survey are obtained by sampling the expenditure patterns at different levels of income in one specific year.

Over time, segments of the population move from lower to higher income groups, changing the total level of demand. It is this movement in demand over time that is of primary concern to the forecaster and, fortunately, its effect is easy to illustrate. Expenditure data on a particular product or class of products can be taken over a period of time and compared with the totality of consumer expenditure. Graph 2.8 shows two differing trends for food and consumer durables. It can be seen that there was a fairly steady decline in the expenditure on food relative to total consumers' expenditure, with only a temporary plateau in the mid 1970s representing any break in the trend. As would be expected, expenditure on durables rose relative to total expenditure; however, because of the cyclical nature of the durables market, the underlying trend is harder to visualise (if needed, trend line estimation can be used). In these two examples, the average annual percentage decline in food expenditure relative to total consumers' expenditure was 2.3% a year; the corresponding increase in durable expenditure was 1.3%. These guidelines can be produced for most product and service groups and provide a benchmark for forecasting purposes, relative to any assumptions being made about economic growth and consumer expenditure.

Although we have moved away from the simple world of single products with some determinable saturation level, the thought processes should be similar. There is often an implicit acceptance that the various income elasticities and the relative growth rates

---

22 *Household Food Consumption and Expenditure 1989*, Ministry of Agriculture, Fisheries and Food.

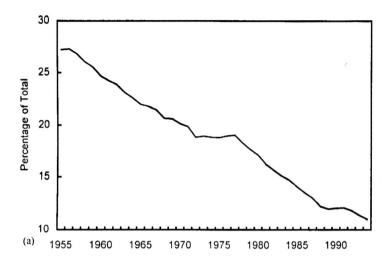

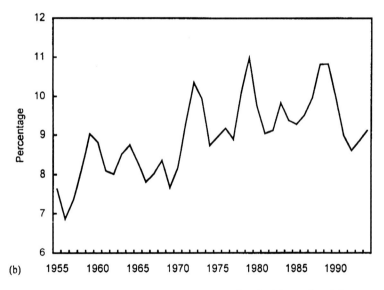

Graph 2.8 Consumers' expenditure: (a) on food; (b) on durables (source: *Economic Trends*).

over time are unlikely to change. However, it is essential to question continually whether there are any factors that are likely to change past relationships. For a start, there can be different elasticities at different levels of national income – food expenditure would rise at low levels of income. External events can also change established elasticities, the temporary impact of Middle East conflicts on air travel being an example.

Capital goods

So far we have discussed consumer goods only. However, we must recognise that many products (e.g. a drop forge or a milling machine) are bought not by the consumer but by businesses with a view to producing consumer goods or for providing a service to consumers (a car wash or a dentist's chair). These are typically called capital goods because they represent the capital used by businesses to produce the products or services that are directly consumed by the final customer. By their nature, capital goods are durables and we will be looking to see whether we can apply the ownership and saturation concepts developed when discussing consumer durables.

It is important to point out now that, as so often happens, the labels used can be misleading. It does not matter a great deal: we all use convenient shorthand labels in conversation and providing everybody knows what is meant it does no great harm, and may even provide peripheral employment for the pedant. However, there are times when one gets so used to the label that one fails to think what lies behind it. So it is with capital goods. There are a number of products where the buyer may be either a member of the public or a business. If the buyer is a consumer then the product is a consumer good; if a business, economically, it is a capital good. The growth in the numbers of self-employed working at home makes the grey area between consumer and capital goods increasingly large. Obvious examples of products that can be both capital and consumer products are the motor car, the personal computer and the telephone. In the economic statistics, my house is classified as capital investment whereas the contents, some of which are older than the house, are regarded as consumer goods.

The service sector – the communal durable

The true capital good is a product that has no value to consumers in its own right but exists only to produce the products that the customer ultimately requires. Thus, the drop forge or the steel rolling mill has no direct utility to the consumer but only has relevance as a means of manufacturing the consumer product. However, there are products that are referred to as capital goods because they are owned by businesses, a reasonable distinction for some purposes, but which in our long term forecasting approach have similarities with consumer durables. ▷**These 'capital goods' exist to provide a service directly to the consumer in the same way as if he had purchased the product himself.**◁ Thus, one might think of dry cleaning equipment which exists solely to provide a service to the consumer in the same way as a domestically owned freezer; or CT[23] scanners, owned by hospitals but supplying a service directly to the public; or a car wash machine, which we discuss later. One can regard these as products that exist primarily so consumers may use them collectively under group ownership rather than use them individually under private ownership.

These 'communal durables', as we might call them, can be subjected to the same analytical process as the consumer durables we have been dealing with earlier. There will be a measurable population of individuals who want access to the product; the growth in that population will be S-shaped; and the rate of change in that S-curve will determine the level of new sales of the product. There is, however, one difference. For the individual, it matters little how often he uses his vacuum cleaner or video recorder; what is economically significant is his decision to become an owner. For the commercial enterprise, what matters is how often the communal durable may be accessed, which, in turn, determines the purchase decision. What we are trying to measure, therefore, is the saturation level of communal use rather than personal ownership.

Earlier in the chapter we showed how, in the absence of detailed statistics, one might approximate the size of a market, and we took haircuts as a consumer example. As another illustration of the thought processes involved in establishing saturation level, we are going to take a service capital good as an example, in this case, car washing machines. There are no reliable figures for the size of this market – what can we do? We do know the size of the car population, 24 million, so the first assumption is the frequency with which owners wash their cars. If we assume the average car

---

23 Computed tomography.

is washed once a month, that would give a daily total of car washes of around 800 000 (24m/30 days). The next assumption needed would be the daily throughput of an individual car wash machine and, for our example we are taking that to be around 120 cars a day. Thus, the maximum number of car wash machines needed, on those assumptions, would be of the order of 7000 (800 000/120). We can then draw up a hypothetical saturation curve in exactly the same way as we did in the consumer section, making our assumptions as to the rate at which saturation level was approached, which in turn gives us a profile of new sales. Graph 2.9, which is based on 90% saturation after 20 years, shows the familiar shape.

It will not have escaped the reader that the only hard fact in the paragraph above is the size of the car pool; otherwise it contained some sweeping assumptions about how often people wash cars and the throughput of car wash machines. This goes to the heart of the forecasting dilemma. ▷ **It is all too easy to run away from the challenge by deriding the assumptions and asserting that the estimates therefore have no value. But, just as it is naïve (or irresponsible) to assume accuracy for a long term forecast based on rough and ready assumptions, so also is it naïve to assume that there is no merit at all in such a prediction.** ◁

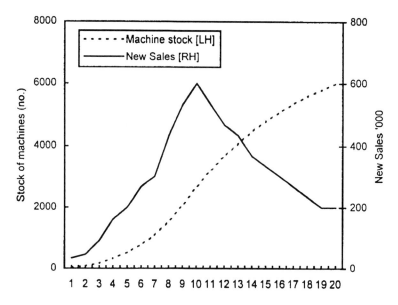

Graph 2.9 Car wash machines – a hypothetical profile.

Even using broadly based assumptions, as above, it possible to do two things, both of considerable value in assessing the future. First, we can establish parameters for our assumptions. For the frequency of car washes, we can postulate a range within which we would not be surprised – say, once a week to once every couple of months. Again, the response of the reader might be that such a range is too wide to be useful – not so. Those (admittedly wide) assumptions would indicate a maximum requirement range from 3500 machines to 14 000 machines; if one is presented with a forecast (and remember we are as concerned with assessing forecasts as with making them) of only 1000 machines or, say, 50 000 machines, we can immediately see that these forecasts require assumptions that we believe to be outside a reasonable range. It does not mean that they have to be wrong, but it does mean that we can go straight to the heart of the forecasting process, isolate that which seems most unlikely, and ask the right questions.

Second, we can remind ourselves that however difficult it may be to quantify the numbers, the levels of usage of the car wash machines and the rate of new sales will have the profile shown in Graph 2.9. We know that the downturn in new sales of machines will come when the use of the product still appears to be in a growth phase; we will be looking for the first signs of weakness in the market, and are more likely to recognise them for what they are and to act on them, than would be the case if we were not aware of the pattern.

Both these points can be reinforced by looking at each end of any range of reasonable expectations; thus, keeping to our car wash example, we can calculate the number of required machines and the annual sales thereof. Graph 2.10 shows the figures for car washing once a week and once every two months. Obviously, the absolute level of machines owned is substantially different, but the pattern of the graph is identical, with the first decline in new sales coming in year 11 in both cases. There is nothing mathematically surprising in that, since the percentage figure for saturation of machines has been kept constant, i.e. the same shaped S-curve has been used in each example. However, simple as this may be, it all serves to concentrate the mind on what we are looking for, and what conclusions we can draw.

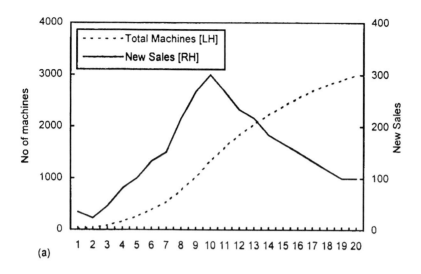

(a)

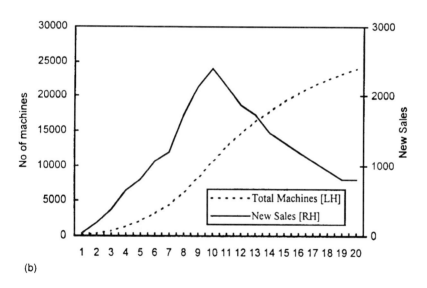

(b)

Graph 2.10 Car wash machines – alternative assumptions: (a) once every two months; (b) once every week.

If we have made the correct assumptions about the length of time needed to reach saturation level, and the rate at which saturation level will be approached, then the fact that we have under- or over-estimated the total size of the market will not prevent us from identifying, in a rough and ready way, the ex-growth point in new sales of car wash machines. At the beginning of the product cycle, the assumptions about the eventual size of the market are probably the most important ones to make. As we move through the product cycle, information on the percentage ownership (or saturation) of the machines is the most important. Indeed, one can be forecasting in an area where statistics are hard to come by but where approximate estimates of ownership are published from time to time. The graphs above clearly indicate that with just a few ownership percentages to hand, a prediction of the timing of the ex-growth point is not too difficult.

The approach used in the car wash example would be directly applicable to any business serving the motor trade – tyre fitting, exhaust centres, service equipment. The skill lies in making realistic assumptions of saturation level and the rate at which it is approached. Judgements will be easier (or harder if one is a pessimist) in some areas than others. The example we used offers far more scope for different opinions on the frequency with which people will want to have their cars washed, if at all, than on many areas of the motor trade – for instance, the need to have tyres changed, where we can use statistics about average mileage and tyre life to estimate the market potential for tyre fitting centres.

Manufacturing capital goods

In turning to what many people regard as 'proper' capital goods – the machines that make the consumer goods – we find that it is much harder to produce practical examples to match our earlier concepts of ownership, use and saturation. Nevertheless, it is once again possible to identify a pattern – this time the pattern of growth in capital goods sales which derives from the underlying growth in sales in the consumer industries being served – and it produces an answer that many people initially find surprising.

In Table 2.7 we start with a theoretical consumer product where the growth rate accelerates and then decelerates. We have assumed a capital to output ratio of 1.5 but that number itself has been chosen arbitrarily – it is just there to remind us that there is a relationship between the stock of capital and output. Forecasters

Table 2.7 Capital goods sales with a variable increase in consumer sales

Year	1	2	3	4	5	6	7	8	9	10	11	12	13	14	15
Consumer sales	100.0	101.0	103.0	106.1	110.4	115.9	122.8	131.4	140.6	149.1	156.5	162.8	167.7	171.0	172.7
% change		1	2	3	4	5	6	7	7	6	5	4	3	2	1
Capital output ratio	1.5	1.5	1.5	1.5	1.5	1.5	1.5	1.5	1.5	1.5	1.5	1.5	1.5	1.5	1.5
Capital stock	150	151.5	154.5	159.2	165.5	173.8	184.2	197.1	210.9	223.6	234.8	244.2	251.5	256.5	259.1
% change		1	2	3	4	5	6	7	7	6	5	4	3	2	1
New capital goods sales		1.5	3.0	4.6	6.4	8.3	10.4	12.9	13.8	12.7	11.2	9.4	7.3	5.0	2.6
% change			102.0	53.0	37.3	30.0	26.0	23.7	7.0	-8.3	-11.7	-16.0	-22.0	-31.3	-49.0

wanting to build in trends towards greater or lesser long term capital efficiency can do so by altering the ratio. Thus, in our example:

- the growth in the capital stock mirrors the consumer product growth rates;
- the size of the capital stock forms the typical S-curve, as illustrated in Graph 2.11;
- the absolute level of capital goods sales falls as soon as there is a decline in the percentage change in consumer sales.

If we look at year 10 in Table 2.7 we see that this is the year that the growth rate in consumer sales falls and the growth rate of the capital stock falls in parallel. However, ▷**once the growth rate in the capital stock falls, the absolute level of new capital goods sales also falls**◁ – see Graph 2.11. This is analogous to the consumer durable examples where, as the growth in the stock of durables falls, then the absolute level of annual sales falls.

Graph 2.11 starts with the capital goods stock (an S-curve replicating the consumer S-curve) and then compares it with the absolute level of capital goods sales (a) and the percentage change in new capital goods sales (b). These graphs illustrate a most important point in capital growth forecasting: continued growth in consumer sales is not sufficient to produce growth in sales of the relevant capital good. ▷**For capital goods sales to continue to increase, the rate of increase in consumer sales must hold level or increase.**

We have already argued in this chapter that claims of never-ending growth in consumer products must be treated with a degree of caution, particularly when they are made for durables; how much greater the caution if we hear such claims being made for capital goods.◁

If such a sharp fall in capital goods sales can be precipitated by no more than a slowdown in the rate of growth in consumer sales, one might ask what happens when consumer sales flatten out completely, or even go into decline. Put simply, ▷**if sales of the consumer product are not increasing then it follows that there is no need to increase manufacturing capacity.**◁ Net capital investment[24] is only required if consumer sales are increasing. Thus, capital goods sales in our theoretical world fall to zero. A fall in consumer

---

24 That is, investment in excess of that needed to replace the existing capital stock.

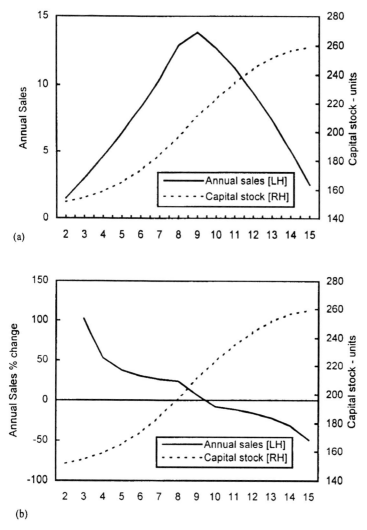

Graph 2.11 Capital stock and capital goods sales: (a) capital goods sales
– absolute; (b) capital goods sales – % change.

sales is more typically a cyclical phenomenon. We will discuss
capital goods behaviour in these conditions in Chapter 3.

It is also worth pointing out that when the consumer product is
a durable, where as we saw, demand was a function of the rate of
change in ownership, the behaviour of the dependent capital good
is even more volatile – yet one more rate of change is introduced.
Readers can prepare their own tables if they so want.

The theoretical examples above obviously represent extremes, in that they assume a specific consumer product with a machine dedicated solely to producing that product. We must now move away from this simplistic (though illustratively important) position and consider two more common propositions:

- Many capital goods are not dedicated – they can produce a variety of different products, established or new. While demand from one customer may be falling, demand from others may be rising.
- The market for many capital goods is the replacement of technologically inferior capital goods and we shall explore this in more detail.

Technological replacement

Where a clearly superior manufacturing process is introduced, forecasting the capital goods demand engendered by technological replacement can be easier. The big advantage is that we know the size of the consumer market and the existing capital stock; all we are trying to do is to estimate the rate at which the new technology will be adopted.

For example, in the glass industry, the float process replaced the previous sheet technology; the size of the glass market was known and, although it was increasing, that was of much less importance than the rate at which the new process was being introduced. Other examples of product-specific technological change include the steel industry's introduction of continuous casting to replace the intermediate use of ingot casting. Technological change that was not specific to one product range includes computer-controlled machine tools.

Table 2.8 illustrates a theoretical profile for a technological replacement of a capital good used in an established consumer market: the consumer market is assumed to be stable at 1000; the capital to output ratio of 1.5 is used as before[25] so the stock of new machines is 1500. An increasing rate of replacement of the old capital stock is assumed, reaching 75% after 15 years. Although the

---

25 To remind ourselves that the link does exist; it may be that in a more sophisticated forecast, we might want to assume a change in the capital output ratio.

Table 2.8 Technological replacement in a stable consumer market

Year	1	2	3	4	5	6	7	8	9	10	11	12	13	14	15
Consumer output	1000	1000	1000	1000	1000	1000	1000	1000	1000	1000	1000	1000	1000	1000	1000
Capital stock	1500	1500	1500	1500	1500	1500	1500	1500	1500	1500	1500	1500	1500	1500	1500
Machine replacement rate (%)	2	4	7	12	18	25	33	41	48	54	59	64	68	72	75
Stock of new machines	30	60	105	180	270	375	495	615	720	810	885	960	1020	1080	1125
New sales	30	30	45	75	90	105	120	120	105	90	75	75	60	60	45

Table 2.9 Technological replacement in a growing consumer market

Year	1	2	3	4	5	6	7	8	9	10	11	12	13	14	15
Consumer output	1000	1030	1061	1093	1126	1159	1194	1230	1267	1305	1344	1384	1426	1469	1513
Capital stock	1500	1545	1591	1639	1688	1739	1791	1845	1900	1957	2016	2076	2139	2203	2269
Machine replacement rate (%)	2	4	7	12	18	25	33	41	48	54	59	64	68	72	75
Stock of new machines	30	62	111	197	304	435	591	756	912	1057	1189	1329	1454	1586	1702
New sales	30	32	50	85	107	131	156	165	156	145	132	139	125	132	116

stock of the new technology machines continues to rise, the level of annual sales declines from year 9, the point at which the percentage increase in the replacement rate declines – a familiar profile.

In Table 2.9, the replacement rate remains the same as Table 2.8, but the consumer market and, hence, the total required capital stock, is assumed to grow at 3% a year. By now, it should be no surprise that, although the total size of the capital goods market is higher than in Table 2.8, if we keep the same replacement profile the decline will begin in the same year (9). The market for the new capital good holds up much better in Table 2.9, and there are even one or two years after the sales peak (year 8) where annual sales still manage a percentage increase – years 12 and 14; this is because the increase in the size of the consumer market is quantitatively greater than the effect of the reducing rate of increase in the replacement rate. Graph 2.12 demonstrates the difference between the stable and the growing markets and ▷**it can be seen that the relationship between the rate of consumer sales growth and the technological replacement rate is crucial to the new sales of capital goods.**◁ Out of interest, to avoid a decrease in new capital goods sales, we need an ever-faster rate of increase in the consumer market the closer one comes to 100% replacement.

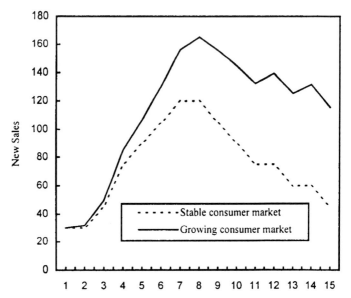

Graph 2.12 Technological replacement.

The illustration used for technological replacement represents an extreme – a completely new machine or manufacturing process that is very substantially superior to the previous generation of machines. It renders the existing machinery technologically, rather than physically, obsolete. However, most technological progress is of a more gradual nature. New equipment represents an improvement on the old but the cost savings are not so great that the manufacturer is commercially compelled to make the investment. The new technology machines are more likely to be bought when the old machines needed replacement; perhaps they accelerate replacement a little, but not to the point where it significantly distorts the replacement process.

A good example of the gradual technological substitution within a broad class of capital goods is provided by the machine tools industry in the 1980s. Basic numerically controlled machine tools were introduced in the 1950s and the first computer controlled tools in the 1960s. The increasing sophistication of the computer control options in the 1980s then created a rapid rate of substitution as can be seen in Graph 2.13: numerically controlled tools rose more or less steadily from 20% to over 50% of the total. Observation of the composition of the non-numerically controlled machine tools shows that the forming tools held steady at around 20% (not surprising as these are dedicated tools, stamping and pressing fixed shapes). Virtually the whole of the gain in market

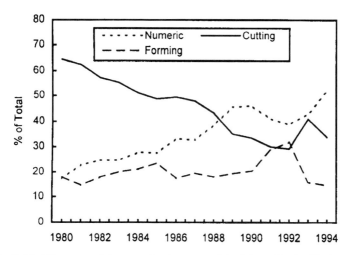

Graph 2.13 New machine tools (source: Machine Tools Technologies Association).

share came at the expense of cutting tools (the non-dedicated tools required for shaping).

Components and intermediates

The whole of this chapter has discussed products as if they were for the ultimate user – consumer products and services bought by the public, or capital goods bought by companies. This (necessarily) simplistic view of commercial life neatly ignores the whole of the production process which incorporates a wide range of components and intermediate products; forecasts are needed for them no less than end products.[26] We can easily find our terminology tied up in definitional knots; however, ▷**we can think of a component as a separate entity in its own right but which forms part of the final product,**◁ e.g. a fractional horse power motor in a washing machine or a clutch in a car. ▷**An intermediate would be material used in manufacture in variable quantity and often changing its form in the process**◁ – here we can instance major industries such as the whole of the steel and non-ferrous industries, plastic polymers, packaging etc.

Having made a rough distinction between components and intermediates to illustrate the range of products and to provide an all-embracing heading, that division will now be abandoned in favour of one that is more useful for the forecasting process. Continuing with our earlier themes, we need to distinguish between *dedicated* and *broad spectrum* products. Dedicated products are, as the name suggests, those that are primarily used by either one or a narrow range of end products, or within one industry classification. Broad spectrum products are those where the customer base is diversified. The forecaster's first task is to see the extent to which the component or intermediate can be linked to an end-product or industrial sector for which forecasts can be made. Thus, we ask if the component or intermediate is used in the capital goods, the consumer durable, or the consumer non-durable markets? Is it predominantly used for new sales; is it a replacement product; or an industrial consumable that wears out in the production process?

---

26 'Intermediate goods industries' accounts for 52% of total manufacturing production.

Some products will be easy to relate to a specific end-user (e.g. tyres for the motor industry), others are obviously very broad spectrum (e.g. electricity supply and distribution). Within that, there are products that are relatively broad in their end-uses but that are predominantly associated with a limited number of customers. Thus, the copper industry's main customers are the electrical and building industries and it is possible to take a specific view of the prospects for their limited range of customers. However, practical experience suggests that once one goes beyond two or three predominant end-users it is better for the outsider to regard the product as suitable for broad spectrum forecasting. The list below translates these generalisations into specific examples.

- **Dedicated products**

Product	Customer industry	Comment
Refractories	Steel industry	Replacement consumable
Fractional horse power motors	Consumer durables (white goods)	New durable sales
Bricks	Housebuilding industry	New building

- **Broad spectrum products**
  Paper and packaging
  Plastic polymers
  Electricity distribution
  Industrial fasteners (nuts and bolts to you)

When earlier discussing broad spectrum consumer products, we referred to income elasticity and suggested that the easiest way to show the relationship between income and expenditure was to prepare a ratio over time – Graph 2.8 showed the relationship between expenditure on food and then durables compared with total consumers' expenditure. The same approach can be used for intermediates.

3 *Playing the cycle*

Summary
The strategies and thought processes involved in forecasting 'cyclical' movements are entirely different from those used in forecasting growth. Cyclical movements take place around a long term trend, whether in growing, stable or declining businesses. It is important to realise that there is not just one economic cycle; the nature of the variety of differing product cycles that exist in the real world must be understood; above all, estimating the turning points in the cycle is of paramount importance.

The chapter opens by dismissing one of the great forecasting fallacies – that some businesses are inherently immune from the economic cycle. After a brief discussion of the causes of cycles, the body of Chapter 3 discusses five different (though often interlinked) types of cycle: the consumer cycle, the stock cycle, the elapsed time cycle, the investment cycle and the replacement cycle. Of these, the elapsed time cycle is the least recognised in the business world.

Chapter 3 concludes by showing how the shape of the cycle may best be plotted and how the forecaster can use the rate of change in the cycle as a signal that a turning point might lie ahead.

The fallacy of the non-cyclical business

We start with a warning. It is convenient to distinguish between cyclical and non-cyclical products or companies; the distinction is particularly important in determining investment strategy at different stages of the economic cycle. Although there are always grey areas in the middle, the differences between a British Steel on the one hand, and a Marks & Spencer on the other, are clearly recognisable. Unfortunately, from that legitimate distinction between comparative responses to the trading cycle stems one of the great forecasting fallacies, which we will call the fallacy of the non-cyclical business. ▷**The fallacy of the non-cyclical business asserts that, because a given business is relatively stable in normal conditions, it is therefore inherently immune to the cyclical fluctuations (usually downwards) that afflict less fortunate companies. Followers of this particular fallacy can be recognised by their supporting statements: 'people must eat'; 'we are all right because we are at the replacement end of the business'; or 'the government funds our business'.** ◁

People do not *have* to do anything in an economic sense, they merely have wants that they pursue to a greater or lesser extent according to their incomes and their priorities. Regrettably, when their incomes come under pressure, people do not have to eat the same amount of food, or of the same quality, or be so relaxed about paying the same price. There is nothing, except a moral or social judgement, that says that a family *has* to have a roof over its head. Similarly, keeping that analogy, the leaking roof that would be repaired immediately in prosperous times may, of necessity, be ignored in recessions while its owner attends to other priorities. The best suggestion I have received for a totally non-cyclical business is crematoria; yet even here the customer, though he cannot postpone the timing of his 'purchase', can at least trade down.

This book has no argument against the distinction between cyclical and non-cyclical companies if the purpose is to differentiate by degree. However, ▷**it would have been better if the term 'less-cyclical' had been deployed rather than non-cyclical, thereby avoiding the implicit assumption that there are businesses that are totally unaffected by cyclical movements.** ◁

Why cycles?

In writing about business cycles, Professor Samuelson stated that 'there have been so many different theories that it has been necessary to devise a number of different systems of classification in which to catalogue them.'[27] Over the years, economic explanations have conflicted, overlapped and not always been easy to understand. This is not an economics textbook and the explanations of the causes of economic cycles can be found elsewhere. What follows is no more than an introduction – but an introduction, nevertheless, from the viewpoint of a forecaster who has had to work with business cycles for over 30 years – and an explanation of the way in which the economic cycle manifests itself.

Cyclicality may arise as a result of an initial disturbance to the underlying trend; once introduced, the cyclical variation will be repeated over time (though with reducing amplitude) even though the original disturbance was non-recurring. The disturbance might well be some external event unrelated to the domestic economy. The examples often cited are war and natural disaster, and the interlinked population movements (e.g. the rise in the UK births after World War II) and one could throw in El Niño and sun spots for good measure. One can also postulate almost any event that changes the trade relationships with other countries: a collapse in the oil price, significant changes in the levels of activity in major trading economies or the emergence of low cost competitive economies. One might distinguish between events that are broadly predictable, in that one can have a basis for anticipating both the timing and magnitude, e.g. movements in the US economy; and those events that might be foreseen as possibilities but are broadly unpredictable as to timing and magnitude, e.g. a collapse in the Russian economy, or a major Los Angeles earthquake.

However, even without the external influences, the national economy has its own inherent cycle. ▷ **If there is a root cause, it is that steady economic growth within the limits of productive capacity appears impossible to achieve. When growth accelerates beyond that which is sustainable in the long term, capacity constraints occur.** ◁ This may reduce exports and increase imports, creating balance of payments deficits. Or it causes bottlenecks and shortages that act as a constraint on output. That in turn would lead to an acceleration in inflation to levels that are deemed to be unacceptable. In either case, the government takes action to slow down the rate of economic growth. Or, in today's open

27 Samuelson, Paul A, *Foundations of Economic Analysis*, 2nd edn, 1983.

international markets, the 'speculators' take action, or the prudent protect themselves, via currency and interest rate instruments. It is a basic axiom of steering any vehicle that if it deviates from course and the driver wants to return to the centre quickly, it is necessary to overcorrect. So it appears with the economy, giving us the familiar stop–go economic cycle.

What is of concern to us in this book is not so much the rationale of the economic cycle as the way in which that cycle manifests itself within specific economic sub-sectors and industries and, in the process, amplifies the secondary effects. A change from economic growth of 3% into a 1% downturn might not, on the face of it, sound unduly serious. Yet a 1% fall in total economic output would be accompanied by substantial falls in the demand for the output of some industries, rarely less than 10% and quite possibly up to 30 or 40%. Indeed, such falls in output can occur without there even being a fall in total economic output – only a reduction in the rate of growth.

Within the general economic cycle, it is possible to identify a number of different industry cycles. Some are obviously related to the broad economic movements outlined above, whereas others are the product of specific events within the relevant industry. In practice, there will be overlap and interaction between the different types of cyclical movement:

- the consumer cycle;
- the stock cycle;
- the elapsed time cycle;
- the investment cycle;
- the replacement cycle;
- the housing cycle could be added since it does sometimes appear to take on a life of its own but the housing market is really an amalgam of the consumer durable and the investment cycles.

The consumer cycle

The consumer cycle is at its most obvious in consumer durables. It has already been made clear that the definition of consumer durables is a matter of degree but they will be recognised as 'large ticket items' and discretionary products with an irregular purchasing pattern; the larger items are frequently bought on credit. Purchasing intentions have been affected in three ways:

- by regulating the terms on which credit can be granted (the hire purchase controls beloved of the 1950s and 1960s policy makers, and now of historical interest);
- the price of credit, i.e. interest rates;
- the confidence necessary to make a large financial commitment is affected by the deterioration in economic activity, or even the anticipation thereof.

There is an implication in some economics books that if it were not for the unexpected external event, then there would be no cycle: not so. It was indicated earlier that government action is normally a response to an economy which is moving out of line with its natural long term trend and in the absence of any government response, the cycle would happen of its own accord.

The principal feature of the economic cycle is not that a 3% increase in output turns into a 1% fall; it is that the change is amplified as the shock waves move through the economy. This happens for two main reasons:

- focusing of expenditure;
- movements in stock levels – discussed separately as the stock cycle.

Consumers concentrate the impact of changing incomes on to a relatively small range of their expenditure. In an economic downturn, consumers suffering a fall in incomes will maintain their expenditure on essentials – food, rent, contractual spending – and reduce their expenditure on entertainment, holidays, cars. The concept of 'discretionary income' describes that which is deemed to be left over after meeting all 'essential' expenditure. Graph 3.1 (a) shows the fluctuations in consumers' expenditure on durable goods compared with their total expenditure. In (b) we amplify the change in total consumers' expenditure so that the almost identical pattern can be more closely observed.

 ▷ **What is essential and what is discretionary can be an interesting debate and forecasters must be wary of applying their own judgement on what they regard as essential to other people's behaviour patterns.**◁ Thus, when asked what ought to be the least discretionary, television rental payments or children's food, most

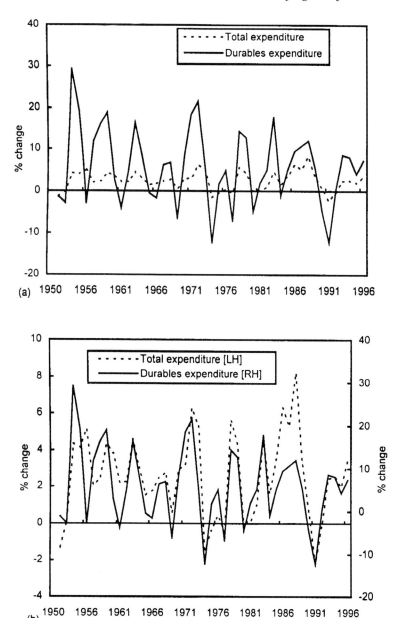

Graph 3.1 The consumer cycle – durables *v.* total consumers'
expenditure: (a) on same scale; (b) to show the pattern (source: *Economic
Trends*).

people would opt for the latter; in practice, it may be the former that holds up better. Judgements on what is, or is not, essential may also vary over time, by social group and according to circumstances. It was always argued that contractual payments, particularly those related to such vital interests as the home (mortgage payments), and one's life (assurance payments), would be maintained at the expense of other elements of the personal budget. Yet the clinking of keys being pushed back through the letterboxes of the building societies when their owners discovered they no longer had a capital asset was matched only by the growth in number of surrendered endowment policies; the supposedly 'essential' payments ceased. ▷**Once again, the forecasting lesson is that you must not assume that what has been true will automatically remain true; the question to ask incessantly is whether any of the factors that made a pattern of behaviour appear immutable have changed.**◁

Although the larger cyclical fluctuations tend to be found in the higher priced durables, the consumer cycle is also apparent in non-durable items and they do not come any less durable than daily press advertising. Graph 3.2 shows the extent to which press advertising amplifies the consumer cycle.

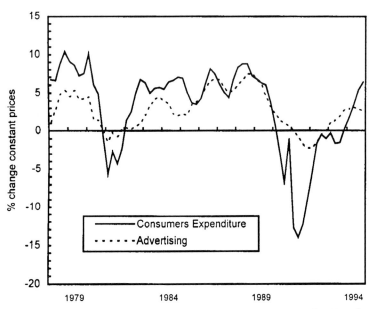

Graph 3.2 Advertising expenditure (source: *Economic Trends; The Advertising Forecast*, NTC Publications, Henley-upon-Thames).

The stock cycle

The second reason why economic change is amplified is because of the production cycle. In a simple world, if demand for cars fell 10%, then everything connected with the car industry would also fall 10%. That it does not lies in stock changes, which have a devastating capacity to create cyclical movements. Indeed, however ably central government managed its economic policy, we would still have stock cycles, albeit of smaller proportions. If there was an economic system that could function without stocks, then a 5% fall in retail demand would instantly convert into a 5% fall in wholesalers' sales, a 5% fall in manufacturers' sales and so on. But as soon as there are stocks, which are primarily a characteristic of manufacturing rather than service industries, buffers are introduced into the flow of goods in exactly the same manner as happens to vehicles on a motorway when the speed limit is reduced from 70 to 50 miles per hour.

Small fluctuations in demand for a product are amplified by changes in stock levels as orders progress through the production and distribution cycle. In Table 3.1, we assume

- an initial 5% fall in consumer sales;
- that all parts of the chain hold stocks equivalent to 40% of their order intake.

Indeed, the snowballing effect can be achieved without the initial level of demand even falling. It may need only a reduction in the

Table 3.1 Stock cycle – the chain effect

	Neutral state	New sales	New stock	% change	Unit fall	Stock % of sales
Retail Sales	100	95		-5	-5	
Stock	*40*		*38*		*-2*	*40.0*
Orders to wholesaler	100	93		-7	-7	
Stock	*40*		*37.2*		*-2.8*	*40.0*
Orders to manufacture	100	90.2		-9.8	-9.8	
Stock	*40*		*36.1*		*-3.9*	*40.0*
Orders to component manufacturer	100	86.3		-13.7	-13.7	
Stock	*40*		*34.5*		*-5.5*	*40.0*
Orders to materials' supplier	100	80.8		-19.2	-19.2	

rate of growth or, making the exercise even more sensitive, a lower rate of growth than had earlier been forecast to induce a reduction in stocks.

Our next exercise is to produce a simplified example of a stock cycle over time showing how each successive stage in the ordering process serves to amplify the initial cyclical fluctuation in retail sales. Graph 3.3 illustrates the starting and finishing cycles to provide an immediate visual impact; the full workings are contained in Table 3.2.

We could have started with the assumption that every enterprise in the chain wishes to keep its stock to sales ratio at exactly the same level, say 20% of quarterly sales, but there is, of course, no requirement for an enterprise to keep its stocks at any fixed percentage of sales – and we have built in some variation in the stock levels. In real life, the stock level decision will reflect

- the current need to service both the flow of production and customers' requirements;
- expectations of what is going to be required in the future.

The variation in stock levels that we introduced to Table 3.2 was predicated on expectations: expectations usually amplify cyclical movements. If the reader wants to follow this through the worked

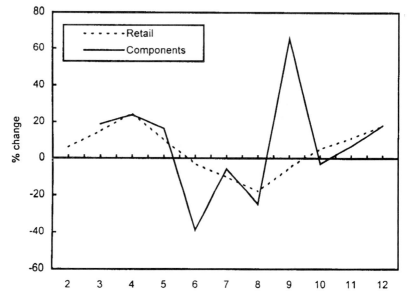

Graph 3.3 Retail and component orders.

Table 3.2 Stock cycle with discretionary stock ratio

Period	1	2	3	4	5	6	7	8	9	10	11	12
Retail sales	100.0	106.0	121.9	152.4	167.6	162.6	146.3	120.0	114.0	119.7	132.9	156.8
% change		*6*	*15*	*25*	*10*	*–3*	*–10*	*–18*	*–5*	*5*	*11*	*18*
Retail stock	20.0	24.4	30.5	33.5	45.0	40.8	25.0	10.0	10.0	15.0	25.0	35.0
Retail orders	100.0	110.4	128.0	155.4	179.1	158.4	130.5	105.0	114.0	124.7	142.9	166.8
% change		*10*	*16*	*21*	*15*	*–12*	*–18*	*–20*	*9*	*9*	*15*	*17*
Wholesale stocks	20.0	22.0	25.5	31.0	38.0	26.0	21.0	15.0	25.0	30.0	32.0	35.0
Wholesale orders	100.0	112.4	131.5	160.9	186.1	146.4	125.5	99.0	124.0	129.7	144.9	169.8
% change		*12*	*17*	*22*	*16*	*–21*	*–14*	*–21*	*25*	*5*	*12*	*17*
Manufacturers' stocks	20.0	22.0	25.5	31.0	38.0	26.0	21.0	15.0	25.0	30.0	32.0	35.0
Manufacturers' orders		114.4	135.0	166.4	193.1	134.4	120.5	93.0	134.0	134.7	146.9	172.8
% change			*18*	*23*	*16*	*–30*	*–10*	*–23*	*44*	*1*	*9*	*18*
Component stocks	20	22	25.5	31	38	26	21	15	25	30	32	35
Component orders		116.4	138.5	171.9	200.1	122.4	115.5	87.0	144.0	139.7	148.9	175.8
% change			*19*	*24*	*16*	*–39*	*–6*	*–25*	*66*	*–3*	*7*	*18*

example then it will go as follows. The retailer will probably build up stock more rapidly as sales increase (peaking in Period 5) and then, when the recession hits, he responds equally dramatically in destocking (see Periods 7 and 8). This amplifies the movement in retail sales as does the subsequent action of the wholesaler ordering from the manufacturer. The manufacturer in turn not only wants to reduce his own levels of finished stock but also the level of his production work in progress; ordering from the component supplier produces a further amplification of the cycle. Thus, in Period 6 of our theoretical example, a 3% decline in retail demand is translated into a 39% fall in component orders. Obviously, the stock ratios chosen are arbitrary, but they are not atypical; the reader can substitute different numbers but the pattern will be the same.

The next point concerns an unexpected, but crucially important point, about the stock cycle. ▷**At the tail end of a recession, the suppliers' activity can sometimes recover before there has been a recovery in retail sales.**◁ To follow this, I am afraid that there is no option but to look at some of the detailed numbers in Table 3.2. In Period 9 there is a 5% fall in retail sales but the destocking has now run out of steam. The retailer has already cut stock to 10 units and can go no lower; so he holds it at 10. However, in Period 8 there had previously been destocking of 15 units but we have seen that in Period 9 destocking is zero. This is a 15 unit improvement which more than offsets the underlying 6 unit fall in retail sales and leads to the retailer ordering 9% more units from the wholesaler. Further down the production line, the wholesaler and the manufacturer actually increase their stocks in amplified response to the retailer's orders.

These worked examples show how, in a period where retail sales fall, we actually have a record percentage increase in component orders. Those numbers are a little arbitrary but the principle is not atypical: ▷**after a long period of falling retail sales, and cumulative destocking, the mere ending of that destocking may be sufficient to create an upturn in activity further down the production line.**◁

We can now move on to another theme, the outcome of which is not immediately obvious: ▷**it is possible to have a stock cycle without there first having been any absolute fall in retail sales.** ◁ This is shown vividly in Graph 3.4 and the workings are contained in Table 3.3.

Table 3.3 Stock cycle with no absolute fall in consumer sales

Period	1	2	3	4	5	6	7	8	9	10	11	12
Retail sales	100.0	106.0	121.9	152.4	167.6	172.6	174.4	175.2	175.2	192.8	221.7	243.8
% change		6	15	25	10	3	1	0.5	0	10	15	10
Retail stock	20.0	24.4	30.5	33.5	45.0	40.8	25.0	10.0	10.0	15.0	25.0	35.0
Retail orders	100.0	110.4	128.0	155.4	179.1	168.4	158.6	160.2	175.2	197.8	231.7	253.8
% change		10.4	16.0	21.4	15.2	-5.9	-5.9	1.1	9.4	12.9	17.1	9.6
Wholesale stocks	20.0	22.0	25.5	31.0	38.0	26.0	21.0	15.0	25.0	30.0	32.0	35.0
Wholesale orders	100.0	112.4	131.5	160.9	186.1	156.4	153.6	154.2	185.2	202.8	233.7	256.8
% change		12.4	17.0	22.4	15.6	-15.9	-1.8	0.4	20.1	9.5	15.2	9.9
Manufacturers' stocks	20.0	22.0	25.5	31.0	38.0	26.0	21.0	15.0	25.0	30.0	32.0	35.0
Manufacturers' orders		114.4	135.0	166.4	193.1	144.4	148.6	148.2	195.2	207.8	235.7	259.8
% change			18.0	23.3	16.0	-25.2	2.9	-0.2	31.7	6.4	13.4	10.3
Component stocks	20.0	22.0	25.5	31.0	38.0	26.0	21.0	15.0	25.0	30.0	32.0	35.0
Component orders		116.4	138.5	171.9	200.1	132.4	143.6	142.2	205.2	212.8	237.7	262.8
% change			19.0	24.1	16.4	-33.8	8.4	-0.9	44.3	3.7	11.7	10.6

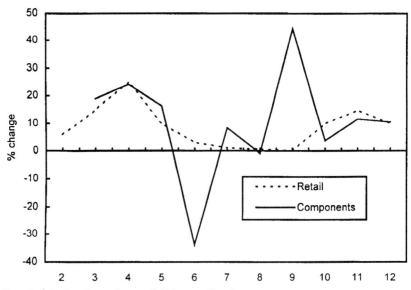

Graph 3.4 Stock cycle: no fall in retail sales.

Having built up stock enthusiastically between Periods 3 and 5 in response to rapidly rising retail sales and the expectation that the good times always roll, the retailer suddenly sees a deceleration in the rate of growth. This engenders a much more conservative attitude to the future in general, and to his stock levels in particular and the absolute level of his stock is cut back. The resultant fall in component orders is at its sharpest in Period 6, with a fall of a third. In that year, the retailer's own sales actually rose by 3% but he reduced his stock by 4 units, having increased it by 11.5 units in the previous year, giving a negative impact of 15.5. units. Even if the retailer had held his stock at the same level as in Period 5, the mere absence of the previous year's large increase in stocks would have been sufficient to cause him to reduce his orders by 3%. ▷ **The crucial element in this exercise was not that his sales fell, but that they did not increase at the rate that he had expected; had the retailer enjoyed perfect expectations, the resultant production cycle would have been more modest.** ◁

The elapsed time cycle

There was a time when economics students were taught about the pig (or hog) cycle, and even the rubber tree cycle, but these no longer feature in the textbooks.[28] Nevertheless, as an introduction to what we have termed the elapsed time cycle, pigs remain a wonderful illustration of one of the most important influences on cyclical behaviour. If you feel that you have no great interest in pigs, do not switch off – the parallels are widespread and the lessons misunderstood.

If we assume that, at some point in time, the price of bacon starts to rise (Belgium invades Denmark, doctors argue it is healthier than fish, or whatever), farmers respond by breeding more pigs. In this case, the buffer between action and effect is not stocks, it is time. Throughout the time that it takes to bring a pig to marketable size, farmers will be responding to the positive price signal. Each farmer will be acting sensibly from his own viewpoint but their actions will be collectively ruinous because, inevitably, too many pigs will be produced and, hence, the price collapses. Even when the price has begun to fall, production continues to increase because farmers part way through the cycle have little option but to complete the breeding process.

So why do they do it? ▷**In part, there is a tendency to assume that whatever is the current state of affairs, it will continue. The present always exerts a greater psychological influence than the future. The memories of the past diminish and the lessons are ignored. The siren call, which tempts all forecasters is 'this time it is different' but it rarely is, and off they collectively go.**◁

But to go back to our pigs, the individual farmer is not necessarily being stupid. If he refrains from increasing production, because he knows that collectively it will be self-defeating, what purpose does it serve him? The other farmers will still increase their output, the price will still collapse and he will have fewer pigs to sell. ▷**So, despite knowing that he is part of an incorrect decision-making process, he still sets out on an economic course that is collectively damaging.**◁ Those who wish to pursue this further can turn to game theory, which is interesting to read, though, at times, mathematically testing. A central tenet of game theory is that if the participants have a perfect ability to consult, and complete trust in the answers received, then optimum decisions will be made by all concerned. To the extent that they cannot consult, or do not have confidence in the veracity of the answers, then each individual will choose the option that causes him the least damage.

---

28 Changes in the structure of the agricultural industry have diminished the force of the pig cycle and the rubber market has long been synthetic based.

In practice, most people do not *know* a decision is wrong, they *think* it is wrong, they *feel* it is wrong with varying degrees of confidence. When their peers, their competitors, perhaps even their colleagues are encouraging expansion, it is very easy to get pulled along. Perhaps sheep would have been a better example.

In so far as the pig cycle is a representation of the effect of delays in response time, the parallels throughout the commercial world are extensive. Examples would be:

- the shipping industry which responds to changes in freight rates by ordering new ships, the delivery of which may take two to three years;
- the property development industry which responds to rising rents and falling investment yields by increasing the number of new development schemes and bidding up the price of development sites;
- mining companies which respond to rising metal prices by increased exploration and opening of new mines;
- manufacturing companies that increase their capital spending at the top of the cycle (see the next section on 'The investment cycle'). Even in industries dominated by only a few producers (with good knowledge of each other's investment intentions) the investment cycle still exists, often accentuated by the desire to maintain market share.

These are the real lessons of the *elapsed time* cycle. Businesses make rational responses to economic stimuli or signals – higher prices, shortage of capacity. Until sufficient time has elapsed, those responses (increased resources) cannot act on the signal (increased price) – so businesses continue to respond to the signal until there is an over compensation.

 ▷ **As a purely personal observation, company managements appear to have a reasonable understanding of the consumer cycle and the stock cycle; much less so with what I have called the elapsed time cycle. It is a rare board that will admit behaving in sheep-like fashion yet that has all too often been the reality.**◁

The investment cycle

Investment, or capital goods, is not required for its own sake but as a means of producing goods that are required by the consumer;

the demand for capital goods is, therefore, a derived demand.[29] Economists refer to the accelerator theory which rests on a fixed relationship between production and investment – the capital output ratio. It will be argued below that, because it is a derived demand, the investment goods cycle will nearly always magnify the consumer cycle to which it relates. The fluctuations in manufacturing investment relative to consumers' expenditure are shown in Graph 3.5.

In Table 3.4, a modest demand cycle for a consumer product has been postulated and the same capital stock of 1.5 times output has been assumed (though that number matters little as it has once again been maintained at a constant level for the purpose of this exercise). As in Table 2.7, the required capital stock will fluctuate in exactly the same proportions as does the output. However, the demand for new investment is derived from the rate of change in the capital stock and in looking at the fluctuations in new investment we are effectively looking at the rate of change on a change. Thus, in years 3 and 4, when the factory output rises by 8%

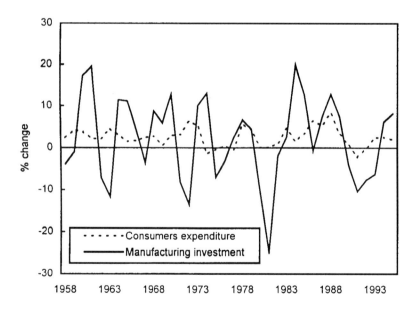

Graph 3.5 Manufacturing investment (source: *Economic Trends*, Govt Statistical Services).

29 We are only considering investment intended to increase capacity; there will also be investment to replace the existing stock or to improve its productive efficiency.

and 11% respectively, this translates into a 50% and 60% increase in new investment. The net effect is also shown in Graph 3.6.

Whereas the initial upswing in the capital goods cycle is merely an amplification of the consumer upturn, the downturn can appear more extreme – and with a skew that affects the nature of the following upturn. In year 5 we have suggested a small reduction in consumer demand, in which event the required

Table 3.4 Simple capital goods cycle

Period	1	2	3	4	5	6	7	8	9	10
Consumer output	100	105	113	125	122	117	115	123	130	138
% change		5	8	11	-2	-4	-2	7	6	6
Capital output ratio	1.5	1.5	1.5	1.5	1.5	1.5	1.5	1.5	1.5	1.5
Required capital	150	157.5	169.5	187.5	183	175.5	172.5	184.5	195	207
Required annual investment		7.5	12	18	-4.5	-7.5	-3	12	10.5	12
Actual investment		7.5	12	18	0	0	0	0	7.5	12
% change			60	50	-100					60

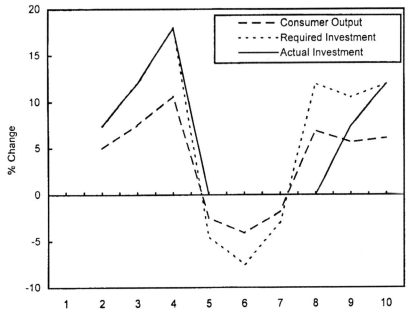

Graph 3.6 Capital goods cycle

capital stock actually falls. ▷**However, it is not feasible to move to that required lower level as the new investment would be negative;** **since it is not normally regarded as sound business practice to take out part of the production line and return it to the manufacturer, in practical terms the level of new investment falls to zero. In our simplistic example, if consumer demand falls there is no need whatsoever for any additional investment.** ◁

While consumer output continues to fall in years 6 and 7, the demand for new investment remains at zero. The interesting year then becomes year 8 when consumer output rises by 7%; new investment still remains at zero because the spare capacity built up in years 5 to 7 has yet to be absorbed. ▷**Because in our simple example we had assumed no disinvestment, there is a lag before new investment can respond to the increase in consumer demand**◁ – hence the earlier comment about the skew in the line.

▷ **It does not need a fall in consumer output to produce a downturn in the capital goods cycle.**◁ The relationships in Table 3.4 were predicated on a clearly recognisable consumer cycle but it is important to understand that a capital goods cycle can result from no more than a slowing down in the rate of growth in consumer demand – and we almost drifted in to this when discussing capital goods in Chapter 2. The observation also relates to the discussion above on the stock cycle – when it only needed a slowing down in the rate of increase in consumer sales to produce a downturn further back in the production process. So it is with the capital goods cycle and we show a theoretical example in Table 3.5.

Of course, Table 3.5 is an extreme position, constructed to a make a particular point. We know from observation that, by and large, capital goods companies do not find that their order intake falls to zero for two or three years and a variety of ameliorating factors

Table 3.5 Capital goods cycle with no fall in consumer output

Period	1	2	3	4	5	6	7	8	9	10
Consumer output	100	102	105	109	114	117	119	120	122	126
% change		2	3	4	5	3	2	1	2	3
Capital output ratio	1.5	1.5	1.5	1.5	1.5	1.5	1.5	1.5	1.5	1.5
Required capital	150	153	157.5	163.5	171.0	175.5	178.5	180.0	183.0	189.0
Required annual investment		3.0	4.5	6.0	7.5	4.5	3.0	1.5	3.0	6.0
% change			50	33	25	−40	−33	−50	100	100

Table 3.6 Capital goods cycle with replacement demand

Period	1	2	3	4	5	6	7	8	9	10
Consumer output	100	105	113	125	122	117	115	123	130	138
% change		5	8	11	−2	−4	−2	7	6	6
Capital output ratio	1.5	1.5	1.5	1.5	1.5	1.5	1.5	1.5	1.5	1.5
Required capital	150	157.5	169.5	187.5	183.0	175.5	172.5	184.5	195.0	207.0
Required annual investment		7.5	12.0	18.0	−4.5	−7.5	−3.0	12.0	10.5	12.0
Replacement demand		11.3	11.8	12.7	14.1	13.7	13.2	12.9	13.8	14.6
Total investment		18.8	23.8	30.7	9.6	6.2	10.2	24.9	24.3	26.6
% change			27	29	−69	−35	63	145	−2	9

will be discussed below. However, do not dismiss Table 3.5 as being totally unrealistic. For single product lines serving single industries, situations not far from that can exist. One can think of kilns for the cement industry, Boeing and the international airline industry, power station turbines, railway rolling stock (RFS Industries, a management buy-out from British Rail, went into receivership in 1993). Where a company is narrowly based, then talk of orders vanishing is not a figure of speech.

 The references so far have covered new investment but, of course, ▷**much investment is of a replacement nature and the existence of replacement demand is one of the principal factors mitigating the severity of the new demand cycle.**◁ Table 3.6 incorporates a non-discretionary replacement rate of $7\frac{1}{2}\%$ of the stock of capital to illustrate the way in which the new demand cycle could be softened. The non-discretionary assumption represents one end of a range of possibilities on replacement, the other extreme being that replacement expenditure is every bit as discretionary as new investment. But even then the upturn in capital goods output is brought forward because the replacement expenditure foregone acts as a form of negative investment.

The importance that replacement expenditure has in the capital goods cycle will depend on:

- The natural life cycle of the product – is it a paper mill lasting 50 years or a grinding tool lasting three months?
- The element of spares – there may be excess capacity within a plant but if the units are not discrete enough to be closed

down, spare parts may be needed to keep the plant working, e.g. rollers on a steel mill.

Leaving aside replacement demand and returning to new demand only, the underlying reasons why corporate behaviour may not mirror the simple model are product range and customer diversity. Even pure capital goods companies (i.e. with no consumer-related products in their portfolio) rarely make only one product. Thus, a company such as GKN has its products including tanks, helicopters, constant velocity joints, industrial pallets and vending machines. Although the economic cycle will tend to depress all capital goods industries, there will be differences in timing which will moderate the individual company's demand cycle. Equally, for the same product there may well be customers in a range of different industries where the timing of their individual cycles will not be identical, e.g. machine tools. Overseas markets will provide even greater cyclical diversity. To take another diversified capital goods company, Smiths Industries makes three-quarters of its sales outside the UK. Its Medical Systems Division manufactures in both the UK and the US and sells additionally into the Far East.

Expectations may damage your wealth

The simple model can be further complicated (or brought closer to reality) by introducing expectations. Expectations of what is going to happen can be as powerful an impact on demand as the underlying relationships and can therefore distort the reality. If the capital stock was infinitely and immediately variable there would be no need to anticipate; capital power could be turned on and off like a driver using accelerator and brake. However, lead times in ordering plant can range from perhaps a few weeks to order and install a new machine tool to several years to build a new production facility. Including the planning process, investments such as power stations can easily take a decade to realise. This takes us back to the elapsed time cycle. Managements plan their investment decisions on the level of demand that they expect to experience rather than the actual level of demand at the time.

Thus, a sharp fall in demand that is expected to be only temporary would not necessarily impact on the investment programme which further serves to moderate the impact of the consumer cycle on the investment cycle.

In contrast, there are occasions where the introduction of expectations can exacerbate the fluctuations in capital spending. For instance, expectations of an increase in the rate of growth in demand from 2% a year to 4% a year it would lead to an increase in investment. If customer demand remains at 2% then that increase in investment will have proved unnecessary; there will need to be a corresponding reduction in capital spending thereby introducing a capital goods cycle solely as a result of incorrect expectations. A classic example of unfulfilled expectations was the reaction of the UK's Central Electricity Generating Board in the 1960s to George Brown's ill-fated National Plan forecasts of a rate of economic growth of 4% a year. The CEGB believed it and embarked on a power station building programme which was to lead to a massive overcapacity and a subsequent collapse in orders.

The UK Labour Government's National Plan, published in 1965, was based on a fundamental ambition: 'Our aim is to step up production so that by 1970 we are producing a quarter more than last year' (i.e. 4% a year). The Plan went on to say that 'The nationalised industries have drawn up investment programmes to provide the fuel … to meet the 25% growth rate .… Heavy investment by the electricity generating boards over the next few years should do away with the overload on power stations'.

In the event, economic growth failed to sustain an annual average of 4%. The period 1964–70 recorded real growth in GDP of 17%, not that much short of the growth rate in the previous six year period. But look at what happened to deliveries of electricity generating plant! Graph 3.7 shows net[30] plant commissioned rising from around 2000 MW a year to a peak of around 5000 MW, and there followed a complete collapse in demand to the point where net commissionings were negative.

---

30 The balance between new plant commissioned and plant taken out of service.

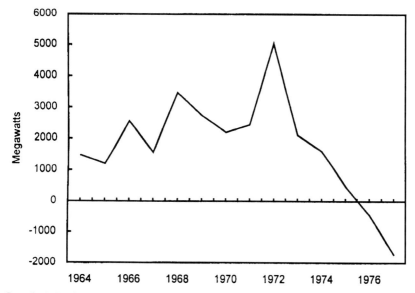

Graph 3.7 Electricity generating investment.

Not all firms go down together

Some companies will be in sectors of the market that are enjoying a secular growth phase such that they will be expanding and investing throughout the general recession. Even within industries that are experiencing a downturn there may be individual companies that are gaining market share to the extent that their output, or at least their expected output, is increasing. If we look at Table 3.4 we see that in year 5 there was a fall in consumer output from 125 to 122, with the result that there was no net investment. Let us suppose that the industry was supplied by five firms in the following manner:

	Year 4	Year 5
Company A	45	41
Company B	35	32
Company C	20	20
Company D	15	17
Company E	10	12
Industry	125	122

Companies D and E, enjoying an increase in output, will need additional investment and, as plant cannot readily be switched from Companies A, B and C to the more successful firms, there will be net new investment over and above that which would apparently be indicated by the industry's overall requirements.

In the early stage of a recession, the reduction in investment plans from the majority of firms that are experiencing lower sales will be significantly larger than the increase in investment proposed by the successful minority. However, when that majority has cut its investment to the irreducible minimum, as per the simple model, they can cut no further. Thus, ▷ **at the end of the downwards phase, the continued investment programmes of the successful minority can lead to a recovery in investment before aggregate demand has recovered back to the pre-recession level of output, i.e. when there is still surplus capacity within the industry.** ◁

Plans and expectations are of no use without the money

Anticipated output is not the only determinant of investment: the level of profitability and the rate of interest on borrowings influences companies' ability to finance investment. This is a particular consideration in both the public (whether it be central and local government or public corporations) and the private sector. The constraints imposed by falling cash flow in a recession are readily understood. Managements' long term view of the desired level of capital stock will take second place to preserving the financial base of the business or staying within overdraft limits. The stimulus provided by cash inflows is not quite as impelling, but it remains powerful. Improved cash flows allow management to resurrect capital spending programmes that had previously been curtailed. Moreover, the existence of surplus capital often leaves managements looking around for something on which to spend it rather than return capital to the shareholder.

The replacement cycle

The expression 'replacement cycle' will be encountered frequently in forecasting but it is not a cycle in the sense that has been discussed so far, i.e. the consequence of a general economic cycle. Rather, the replacement cycle relates to distortions in the long term trend of demand that result from earlier distortions in the sale of original equipment. If a product with a physical life cycle of around ten years quickly achieves high levels of ownership, then original equipment demand will tail off but in, say, years 9 to 11, there will be an upswing in demand due to product replacement. Given that there is flexibility on the timing of replacement purchases, the impact of the original bunching of sales will be dissipated but there would probably be another upswing in replacement demand centred around year 20. A replacement demand cycle can also be triggered, not by the original introduction of a product, but by distortions to the pattern of original equipment purchases. Thus, if there is a boom in car sales as a result of economic stimulation then in, say, a further five years' time there could be an increase in replacement sales.

That is the replacement cycle in its pure form but if you remember the 'fallacy of the non-cyclical business', we can extend that to replacement. ▷**The 'need' to replace a product is strongly influenced by the ability to afford that replacement. The timing of** **much replacement has a discretionary element to it and in a depressed economy there will be a tendency to hold back replacement purchases**◁ – if that were not the case, the motor industry would scarcely have a cycle. Keeping to the motor industry, if the 'lid' is kept on replacement demand for too long, and the average vehicle ages and becomes more expensive to maintain, the discretionary element in the timing of replacement reduces and there can be what is almost a forced increase in replacement demand even though there had been no underlying economic recovery.

The shape of the cycle

When the absolute data for a cyclical product are plotted, the shape of the cycle will usually be apparent, but it will not always stand out. In particular it can be difficult to identify the turning points, where we are looking at the rate at which demand is changing. As will have been seen in some of the earlier graphs, the rate of change has been shown more clearly by plotting not the absolute figures but the percentage change against the comparable period in the previous year. In Graph 3.8 we return to an earlier example of an industrial cycle – that of press display advertising. This time we show both the absolute quarterly figures for display

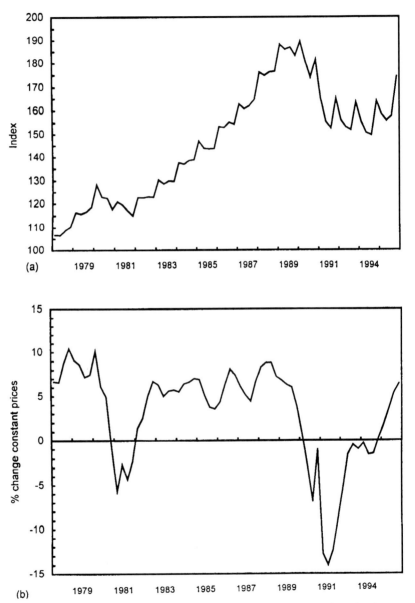

Graph 3.8 Display advertising: (a) absolute figures; (b) % changes (source: *The Advertising Forecast*, NTC Publications).

advertising and that same data plotted as a percentage change compared with the same period in the previous year .

It is a mathematical truism that, before a recession can end and a positive trend emerge, the rate of decline has to diminish to zero. Looking at the right hand graph, for instance, we can see the percentage change graph bottoming out at –14% in the second quarter of 1991, then rising steadily until it crosses the line and becomes positive in the fourth quarter of 1993. Of course, between those two dates, the absolute level of demand for display advertising is getting worse; the third quarter of 1993 may even produce newspaper headlines such as 'lowest quarterly display advertising for seven years'. Yet all the time the rate of decline is diminishing and, again by definition, the lowest absolute point is the very time that demand is poised to recover.

The previous paragraph seeks to do no more than point out that it is easier to identify a cyclical turning point by looking at a graph of percentage changes than by looking at the absolute figures. The forecaster will be looking for such patterns to alert him to a potential turning point in the cycle. Although it is true that there cannot be a recovery without there first being a reduction in the rate of decline, it is not the case that a reduction in the rate of decline must *necessarily* be followed by a recovery.

We can take a further look at the graphs for display advertising, this time over a shorter time period (Graph 3.9). By the first half of 1993, the steady fall in the rate of decline in display advertising meant that the 'recovery' in the percentage change had virtually reached the zero line: the 'pattern' was suggesting the imminent emergence of a positive percentage change, i.e. a recovery in the absolute level of advertising. However, as the graph shows, there was some hesitation in the recovery and the forecaster would need to decide whether it was actually going to happen. This illustrates the delicate balance between using these cyclical percentage change graphs as

- a clearer way to demonstrate what is actually happening; and
- a predictive tool.

On this occasion, the forecaster would have been assisted by the right hand graph which showed that the recovery in consumer spending, to which display advertising had been closely linked, had already happened. The forecaster's thought process should be along the following lines:

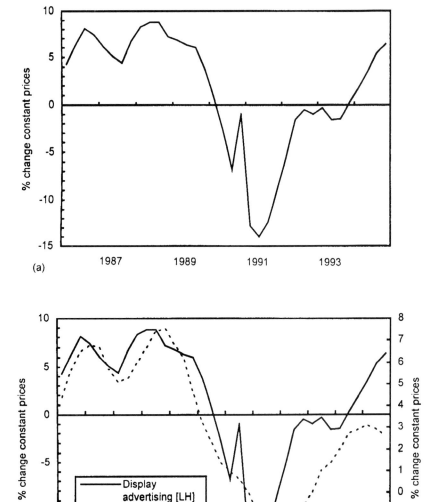

Graph 3.9 Display advertising: (a) advertising only; (b) advertising and consumers' expenditure (source: *The Advertising Forecast*, NTC Publications).

- I know that display advertising is cyclical and that it is closely related to the consumer cycle.
- I can see that the graph is showing a classic recovery pattern.

- I can check that this is consistent with my assumptions for consumer expenditure.
- Having considered whether there are any factors which might be different this time, I will predict with reasonable confidence a recovery in display advertising.

Caution is always needed: a sharp change in the rate of increase or decline is only one of the preconditions for a reversal in a cyclical trend. There are no magic formulae in forecasting and the forecaster still has to think, and to exercise his judgement. ▷**The percentage change graph puts the forecaster on red alert that a cyclical turning point might be on hand; it does not act as a substitute for analytic thought.**◁

It should also be recognised that there are conditions where the percentage change graph does not help much. If an industry has suffered a very prolonged decline, or if demand has fallen very rapidly, the rate of decline must of necessity moderate. In those circumstances it is difficult to tell the difference between an industry that is settling down to permanently lower levels of demand and one that is about to enjoy a cyclical recovery. The UK motor cycle and shipbuilding industries provide depressing examples of long term decline.

You can lead a horse to water

Each type of cycle will have its own characteristics and it is important to be aware of these when trying to anticipate potential turning points. Thus, cycles in consumer durables and discretionary products are easier for governments to send into recession than into recovery. If it is determined, a government can set interest rates at a sufficiently high level to break any consumer goods boom – however high confidence happened to have been. However, equivalent reductions in interest rates do not necessarily stimulate demand if the underlying confidence is absent – however low the rates fall. That is not to say that official policy to stimulate a recovery in consumer goods spending may be totally ineffective; rather that the recovery can take an unconscionably long time in coming.

An excellent example of the difficulty of stimulating a cyclical recovery can be found in the housing market between 1988 and 1993. Interest rate increases to 15% eventually choked off one of the strongest post-1945 booms but repeated reductions in rates to $5\frac{1}{2}$% in 1993 failed to have the normal impact because consumer confidence had been severely dented by the capital losses made on recently purchased properties. Graph 3.10 shows the relationship between housing 'affordability', in which interest rates play a significant role (both directly, and indirectly through their effect on house prices), and transactions in the housing market. The relationship between housing affordability and the number of transactions (i.e. purchases) had been a close one over the years but between 1991 and 1993 it proved singularly difficult to lead the housing horse to the water of recovery.

While recognising that it may be more difficult to engineer a recovery than a recession, there are cycles that have a built in stabiliser. We have already seen that there are conditions when demand at the end of the production chain can recover even before there has been any recovery in consumer demand – an apparent

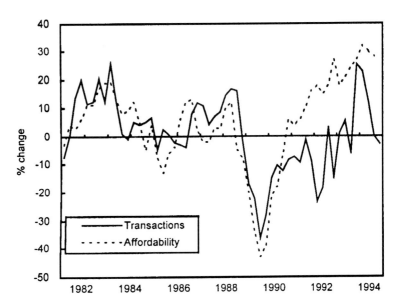

Graph 3.10 Housing transactions (source: *Economic Trends; Private House-Building Statistics*, National House Building Council).

paradox seemingly designed to confuse forecasters. We saw this in the stock cycle and the investment cycle, too, has an built-in recovery element.

Leading indicators

▷ **Recognisable patterns of cyclical behaviour are essential for successful short term forecasting but if you wait until the relevant statistics have been published, your forecast may be correct, but it will not be leading the field.**◁ There are occasions when observation of a reducing rate of decline may be a sufficiently advanced indicator but the successful forecaster is more likely to be predicting the events that normally create a cyclical turning point. For example, a significant change in interest rates, or in taxation will affect the demand for consumer durables. We might describe the changes that typically cause cyclical turning points as trigger events and the final stage of forecasting would be to concentrate on forecasting the circumstances in which a trigger event is likely to occur. Thus, to take one of our earlier examples, a high level of unemployment might suggest tax cuts or a reduction in interest rates which will in turn lead to a recovery in consumer spending and then to press advertising.

Part II

The company

4 Market share

Summary

Chapters 2 and 3 took the reader through various approaches appropriate for forecasting industrial trends, both long term and cyclical. It is now time to move closer to the companies. Between the industry's sales and the individual corporate performance lies the market share.

By definition, the volume of industry sales equals the combined sales of all the companies within that industry. There are forecasters who assume that what happens to the industry, happens to the company. Indeed, in the absence of any other information, it is not an unreasonable starting point. Thus, if the total number of people aged over 80 is showing long term growth, then all nursing homes for the elderly will show long term growth. Or, if the motor industry is coming out of recession, then all motor distributors will show a sharp short term increase in sales. These are simplistic generalisations which, on occasion, may be true enough for our purposes in this time-starved existence: but not always – particularly as the time horizon lengthens.

After opening with some dramatic examples of changing market shares, Chapter 4 asks what we mean by market share; a simple question but with a complicated answer. Markets are not as homogeneous as they sometimes seem to the outsider and we will illustrate the impact of movements in sub-sectors, showing how this can help forecast overall market share. This leads naturally on to management's ability to influence its position within its industry and, equally important, its ability to determine what markets it is in. The chapter finishes with a discussion of one of the most interesting ways in which market share can change – 'cherry picking'.

The speed of change

Market share may be of lesser importance within cyclical analysis than in considering the long term. That is not to say that it is irrelevant, but the timing and pace of cyclical movements in demand are more likely to be the main influences on short term profitability. In the long term, however, changes in market share can be even more important than the overall growth in the relevant industry: the examples below are taken from three mature industries – housebuilding, newspaper and motors. Indeed, the speed with which market share changes can be startling.

In Graph 4.1 the rise and fall of two of the three largest housebuilders is plotted alongside the growth of what had been one of the smaller companies; the lower graph shows two spectacular rise and falls. Graph 4.2 shows the dramatic rise of the *Sun* newspaper (previously the *Daily Herald*) in the 1980s and the decline in the *Daily Mirror* and the *Daily Express*. The final example relates to the passenger vehicle industry, or cars as the layman would have it. Graph 4.3 shows, at the top, the inexorable decline in sales from the UK manufacturing base, with imports increasing their share of the total market from only 8% in 1967 to 56% some 12 years later. On the lower graph we see the related decline of British Leyland within the space of no more than a single decade, relative to the industry as a whole and Ford in particular.

The reason for showing these historic market share graphs is solely to demonstrate the extent to which change can occur between companies in the same industry and to indicate the importance of assessing probable future changes in market share when forecasting for individual companies.

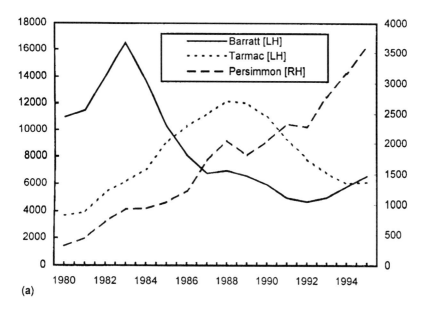

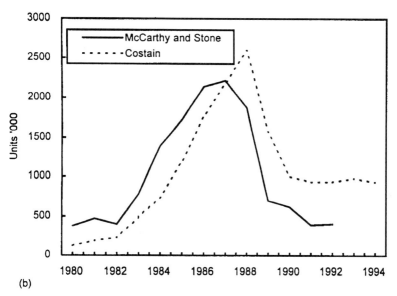

Graph 4.1 Housebuilding industry: (a) housebuilders' unit sales; (b) the rise and fall of ... (source: Credit Lyonnais Laing, *Annual Housebuilding Review*).

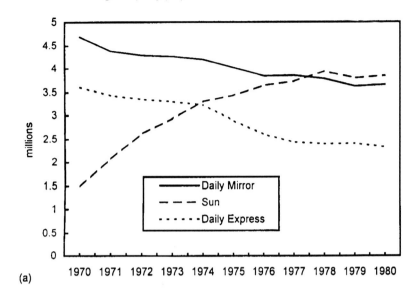

(a)

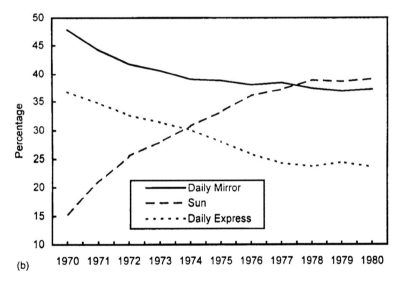

(b)

Graph 4.2 Newspaper industry: (a) newspaper circulation; (b) market share as % of three titles (source: Audit Bureau of Circulations).

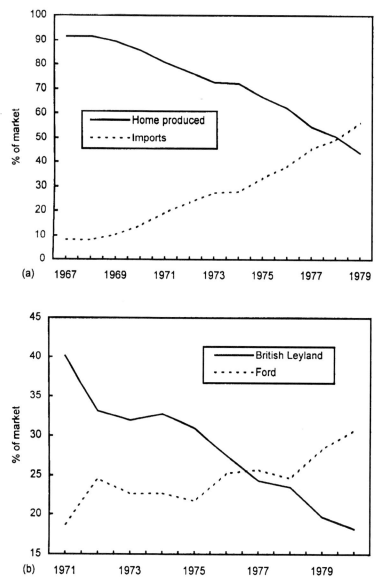

Graph 4.3 Passenger vehicle industry: (a) home production *v.* imports; (b) British Leyland *v.* Ford (source: Society of Motor Manufacturers and Traders).

What do we mean by market share?

Before we talk about predicting market share, we need another digression: what do we mean by market share? Writers often discuss market share as if the boundaries of any particular market were clearly defined. However, as soon as there is anything other than perfect competition, as soon as there is any degree of product differentiation, then we find that there is no clear basis for distinguishing between market share and industry performance – if one chooses to define the industry or sector narrowly enough. If we were pursuing our earlier newspaper example, we can legitimately compare a particular title's circulation with the total newspaper market; alternatively, we might want to distinguish between the popular and quality papers (if such distinction is valid). It is perfectly reasonable to look at the *Daily Telegraph*'s share of the total newspaper market but a more relevant test of its immediate success would be a comparison against the *Guardian*, *Independent* and *The Times*.

We could take a different example, thereby throwing up another interesting paradox. In Table 4.1, we have a hypothetical computer company, manufacturing both mainframe computers and personal computers. ▷ **Its market share is increasing in both mainframe and personal computers, yet its total market share is falling: why? The answer lies in the fact that its starting market share is low in the fast-growing sector and high in the slow-growing mainframe sector.** ◁

Table 4.1 Hypothetical computer market share

Year	1	2	3	4	5
Industry output					
Mainframe computers	100	100	100	100	100
Personal computers	100	120	144	173	207
Total	200	220	244	273	307
Company market share %					
Mainframe	*60*	*61*	*62*	*63*	*64*
Personal	*10*	*11*	*12*	*13*	*14*
Company output					
Mainframe	60	61	62	63	64
Personal	10	13.2	17.3	22.5	29.0
Total	70	74.2	79.3	85.5	93.0
Total market share %	*35.0*	*33.7*	*32.5*	*31.3*	*30.3*

In the short term, companies cannot change the industry or sub-sectors they happen to be in (or in which previous generations of management happened to leave them). In practice, market share will be a mixture of trends within industry sub-sectors and of the company's performance relative to its peers. The greater the degree of product homogeneity, the more relevant will be market share as a concept within the control of the individual company. So, to return to the example above, would you describe our hypothetical computer company as gaining or losing market share, or just being in the wrong place at the wrong time?

Forecasting market share introduces yet one more uncertainty into the total forecasting equation, and one that does not lend itself to systematic analysis. To simplify the task, the forecaster should ascribe as much of the relative performance between firms as possible to differences in product range. For example, is the paper company in newsprint or in coated paper; or is the brewery more concentrated in beer or lager. This will enable the forecaster to draw some initial conclusions about market share before becoming judgemental.

Nevertheless, one is left with the fact that some companies will

- perform better than their competitors for any given range of products; and
- redefine their product areas to take full benefit of changes in industry trends more quickly than do their competitors – in other words part of their management skill will be to get themselves into the right sub-sectors of their industry. No better example could be found (commercially, if not socially) than the repositioning of Labour's one-time flagship, the *Daily Herald*, into the downmarket *Sun*.

Is the playing field level?

Market share may change because the playing field is not level, e.g. costs of production are different. The most obvious example is competition from abroad where foreign manufacturers may have access to lower cost raw materials, cheaper labour or government subsidies. They may, of course, simply operate on a larger scale and be more efficient – long term shifts in relative trade flows are well recognised. In the UK there has been a decline in the share of

trade held in manufactured goods, particularly the traditional
industries. Whether there was an inevitability about the loss of
market share that has been seen in some industries is beyond the
scope of this book. In some areas it has been almost total (motor
cycles, shipbuilding, cameras and wristwatches) and other
industries have seen large parts of their markets go to foreign
suppliers (textiles, zippers and cars). The success that has been
enjoyed subsequently by the Japanese car plants in the UK
suggests that management plays more of a role than the
protectionists care to admit.

A key difference between losing market share to domestic
competitors and losing it to international competitors is that in the
former case, management has the capacity to react positively; in
the latter case, international competition, the playing field may not
be level and there will be circumstances where, however good the
domestic management is, it cannot compensate for the differential
labour costs, raw material advantages, subsidies, the climate, or
whatever. ▷ **Thus, when looking at a company that has suffered a
loss of market share, it is important to form a view on whether that
loss is attributable to intrinsic weaknesses within the corporate
structure – which means that the company may have the capacity to
regain its market share; or whether the loss in market share has
been due to production cost differences beyond its control, in which
case there may be an inevitability about further losses in market
share.** ◁

It is always possible that the international playing field may
also be uneven in favour of UK manufacturers because of
government support, or barriers to entry, both formal and
informal. The forecaster must be aware of the extent to which his
companies are artificially protected and decide whether that
protection is under any threat. It may be possible changes in tariff
levels; it could be government regulation e.g. the protection that
used to be afforded to the UK National Coal Board; or changes in
European Union (EU) rules opening up public sector construction
contracts to continental competitors. Less easy to identify, but
no less important, are the changes in technology which might
permit competition in areas hitherto thought to be protected, e.g.
the impact that computers are having on competition within the
financial services industries.

Management

If you isolate the changes in market share that derive from possessing different product portfolios and from competition based on different cost structures, you are left with that most obvious of explanations for changes in market shares – the quality of management. Related to management quality will be the strength of the firm in a whole variety of areas – technical know-how, brands, finance, etc. These are related to management because they have not (generally) arrived there on their own. However, these advantages are not necessarily derived from the existing management but may be the product of some past management team. Without in any way detracting from the current management of Marks & Spencer, how many generations have combined to produce the unique brand image that now underpins its market share? Reverting to the general, once technical, marketing and financial strengths have been achieved, they may enable lower quality management to sustain market share in the face of competition from ostensibly better management in competing firms but which lack the specific historic strength. Similar support for market share derived from past management achievements might be a patent on the best technology or a monopolistic market position.

The argument can, of course, work in the opposite direction in that the dead hand of the past can hinder even the best of managements. The steel company situated where the coal seams are exhausted, the iron ore deposits depleted and the port not deep enough to take today's bulk carriers may have problems that are insoluble by any management – another version of the level playing field problem. There are structural changes that happen regardless of any management decisions. P&O management can hardly be blamed for Eurotunnel's decision to create additional cross-channel capacity.

▷ **Management ability does not exist in isolation; it has to work within both what it has inherited, which is neither to its fault or credit, and it has to work with what it is able to create itself.**◁ You must try to distinguish between the two. If new management comes in to a company that has performed poorly, but your analysis indicates that the reasons for the poor performance are irremediably structural, then you will not be forecasting a sustained improvement in that company's performance relative to its peers – domestic or international. The same thought process will apply when you look at a take-over and try to assess whether new owners can improve the company's market position. Warren Buffet addressed the industry *v.* management decision in his usual pithy manner: 'When a management with a reputation for brilliance tackles a business with a reputation for poor fundamental economics, it is the reputation of the business that remains intact'.[31] The same point has been made in a more academic context. John King's book, *Foundations of Corporate Success*,[32] provides interesting case studies and general theories as to why certain types of business and management structures are successful, i.e. increase profitable market share. While recognising the importance of inherited market strengths, he rightly warns that 'Strategic assets are often less secure than distinctive capabilities'.

Consistent corporate growth in market share can always be recognised; even if it cannot always be fully explained, it is still legitimate to accept that a successful formula exists, that it represents the product of a superior management team. The working assumption must be that the formula continues, though the forecaster will be continually testing the proposition. Has the 'soft' part of the market now been acquired (see cherry picking)? Has the business reached a size where it is harder to manage?

Firms' collective management ability has to be judged entirely differently by outsiders than by insiders. You do not work with them; you do not see them in action in their own operational environment. Try judging the people who run your own organisation; it is not always easy to decide who is doing a good job and who is not. It can even be difficult at times to work out who is actually making the decisions. So, it must be with all humility that you as an outsider express an opinion on the management of a company with which you have had only the barest of contact.

The outsider will derive his opinion of the management from:

- Meetings – in which the management is seen out of its operating context and sometimes judged more by its ability to communicate than its substantive actions. The finance director, who has no line responsibility, will usually be the main point of contact.

---

31 Berkshire Hathaway Inc., 1985 Annual Report.
32 King, J A, *Foundations of Corporate Success*, Oxford, 1993.

- The company's financial performance, i.e. the results speak for themselves. However, as we have already indicated, these results may owe more to the business the management has inherited than management's own ability. Comparative analysis of results between companies will be an important part of the judgmental process.
- Comments by third parties, usually competitors who have a better basis on which to make a judgement, or the trade press, or even other forecasters, all of which contributes to the received wisdom on management ability.
- Observation of management's business decisions which can be judged against your assessment of rational corporate behaviour, e.g. increasing manufacturing capacity at the peak of the cycle; or a questionable acquisition. However, it is not always easy to attribute credit or blame: who, at British Gas, for instance, was responsible for agreeing the onerous North Sea Gas contracts?

'Cherry picking'

So far, we have been discussing the change in market shares that can occur within the established cast list of players. However, some of the most dramatic shifts in fortune can come from new entrants to a market-place, led by managements with no loyalties to historic structures and practices. One of the characteristics of growth in market share by new entrants is 'cherry picking' whereby a newcomer targets the best cherries, in this case the highest return segments of the market. For cherry picking to be successful, the established market leaders must practise a degree of average pricing. In other words, the product or service must have a broad pricing structure (or price bands) that does not properly reflect the marginal cost of supplying that product to each individual customer (or group of customers). Thus, there is cross-subsidisation between customers. As the Chairman of Royal Bank of Scotland succinctly put it: 'Our strategy is to aim for fat underbelly products.'[33]

Standard examples of cross-subsidisation derive from geographic distribution costs. The Post Office charges the same price

33 *Financial Times*, 9 May 1996.

to send letters throughout the country whatever the relevant distribution cost. So obvious is the potential reward for any potential competitor that wished to charge less for large intra-urban delivery areas than the national rate, to the detriment of the hills and valleys, that the Post Office's national distribution of low cost mail is protected by legal monopoly.

Within manufacturing, a new entrant may concentrate on fast-selling standard lines, selling to customers prepared to take advantage of lower prices on these items, those customers returning to the traditional supplier for the slower-moving stock. All organisations that regard themselves as under an obligation (whether it be legal, or out of a sense of responsibility, or from pride) to offer a comprehensive service, may be vulnerable to the cherry picker.

The success enjoyed by the cherry picker depends on the structure of the particular market and the ability of the potential customer to assess the status and reliability of the new entrant to the market. Thus, cherry picking will be more likely to succeed where

- the customer can evaluate the product – a discount store selling branded products;
- the cost of being wrong is not high in relation to the money being spent – which is why large construction companies always proved reluctant to purchase very cheap East European cement;
- the new entrant's credibility is derived from a well-known large parent – the Prudential is more likely to succeed with a new bank than this author.

Mercury's attack on British Telecom's business users is a straightforward example of cherry picking. A more complex assault on a market, in which cherry picking played a key role, has been provided by the motor insurance industry where the direct telephone insurers, and Direct Line in particular, had captured 25% of the market by 1994 – see Table 4.2. Apart from the advantages of a lower cost base, Direct Line and its followers deliberately targeted the low risk part of the market, refusing even to quote for certain classes of customer, and used postal code data to break down, and then price, geographic claims experience in more detail than the traditional insurers. The ability to cherry pick was enhanced by computer systems that could price more

Table 4.2 Motor insurance premiums (£m)

Annual premiums	1990	1991	1992	1993	1994
Industry	3080	3866	4317	5206	5201
Direct share (%)	12	13	16	20	25
Direct premiums	370	503	691	1041	1300
Increase in direct premiums		133	188	350	259

Source: Association of British Insurers: *General Insurance Sources of Business*, Table 2.

accurately and be more responsive to changes in underlying risk. We will return to this example in Chapter 7.

There are, of course, natural limitations to growth via cherry picking. Niches are, after all, what they mean and the cherry picker must eventually decide whether to remain in his niche or expand across the broad range of the market-place. It may be that the momentum of a growing market share has created a high overhead recovery and a low cost base relative to the traditional suppliers which enables the niche player to take the high ground as well. However, that may also be the point at which the established suppliers reorganise their own businesses and seek to regain lost market share.

Cherry picking represents a very particular example of a focused attack on a market-place, the feature being the concentration on those parts of the market where there has been overpricing. There can, of course, be focused attacks on a market that do not rely on the exploitation of mispricing, merely the selection of a particular point of entry and a determined assault on that entry point. A typical example would be the Japanese approach to some of their export markets. A concentration on a cheap but reliable entry point product in first motor cycles and then passenger cars was designed to create a market presence in markets where, for historic reasons, there may have been a reluctance to buy Japanese. Having established their base, the Japanese manufacturers then moved steadily upmarket, slowly increasing their market share. ▷**Beware the managements who proclaim: 'We are safe, we are at the quality** **end of the market.'**◁

5 *Sources of information*

Summary

Before we move on to the specifics of the company forecast, we need information, hard facts, to enable us to construct the building blocks for whatever forecasting model we decide to use. Early in Chapter 1, we had a heading 'You already know how to forecast'. The message of the section was that the forecasting process itself, the actual exercise of judgement, could be relatively quick; what takes the time is acquiring the necessary information. Chapter 5 takes us through the sources of information open to the outsider preparing a simple forecasting model.

The primary source of information for a profits forecast is the company's annual report, which contains the actual numbers we are trying to forecast. However, accounts are designed for statutory and reporting purposes, not to disclose the economic reality and we discuss the problems of trying to use the content of the profit and loss account to distinguish between fixed and variable costs. The balance sheet is normally used to gauge the company's financial health, but we see that it can also provide us with information about the structure of the business.

The middle part of the chapter looks at the wide range of non-statutory information that is available to the outsider – from the company, from regulatory sources, from competitors and so on. We finish with a world that may only be familiar to the professional forecasters of the investment community – the cosy contact that exists between the quoted companies and financial analysts.

The annual report

This chapter is a prelude to constructing a simple forecasting model. It should go without saying that the first step in modelling any company's profit profile is to draw on whatever information can be obtained from the annual report of the subject company; after all, what we are trying to forecast is the numbers that will be presented in future annual reports. Forecasters will have to decide, according to their own purposes, on which particular number, or combination of numbers, they want to concentrate – be it trading profits, pre-tax profits, earnings per share or cash flow.

The annual report contains the accounts themselves, the content being prescribed by law and professional accounting standards – hence the expression statutory accounts. Additional non-statutory information may also be provided in the annual report ranging from more detailed accounting data to descriptions of the business and explanations of trading performance. We will look first at the statutory accounts, particularly the profit and loss account for this is not only an important source of information – as we have said, it contains the very numbers we are trying to forecast.

For our purposes, it is a passing irritation that statutory accounts are not presented in one standard format. The 1985 Companies Act allows a choice of four formats, though, in practice, only two will normally be found in quoted companies. Format 1 (Table 5.1) would show the turnover, a cost of sales and a smaller figure for other operating expenses, overheads or varying descriptions of distribution and administrative costs. This equates roughly to a division between direct and indirect costs and the costs (e.g. wages) are allocated according to their function.

Using the notes to the accounts, one can obtain important additional information: the amount of total employee costs; of

Table 5.1 Profit and loss format 1		
Turnover		100
Cost of sales	65	
Gross profit		35
Operating expenses	20	
Operating profit		15
Interest paid	3	
Pre-tax profit		12

Forecasting company profits

depreciation and related payments; and sometimes (but not always) of raw materials. Unfortunately, however many pages are occupied in the accounts by the notes, the forecaster will still be left looking at large chunks of costs that are unexplained. Moreover, this disclosure of costs cuts across the earlier division between cost of sales and operating expenses. For example, some of the employee costs will relate to the 'cost of sales' and some will relate to the 'other operating expenses'.

We can look at a practical example, Delta's accounts for 1996. From the face of the profit and loss account we have the figures in Table 5.2. This allows us to break down Delta's published operating profits in the alternative ways (Table 5.3).

Thus, even at this early stage in constructing a model using accounts information, we can choose a breakdown based on either:

- direct costs and indirect costs (or cost of sales and operating expenses); or

Table 5.2 Delta plc accounts 1996

£m		1996*
Turnover		950.0
Cost of sales	(732.1)	
Gross profit		217.9
Distribution costs and administrative expenses	(165.5)	
Operating profit		52.4
Share of profits of associated companies	14.7	
Interest	(9.9)	
Profit before taxation		**57.2**
* Before exceptional items		
Note: 3 *Employee Costs*	241.1	
5a *Depreciation*	31.8	

Table 5.3 Alternative profit breakdown

Direct v. indirect costs	£m	%	By cost category	£m	%
Sales	950.0		Sales	950.0	
Direct costs	732.1	77	Employment costs	241.1	25
Indirect costs	165.5	17	Depreciation	31.8	3
			Other costs	624.7	66
Operating Profit	52.4		Operating Profit	52.4	

- employment expenses, depreciation and whatever is left,

but not both.

Format 2 abandons the distinction between the purpose of the cost (i.e. cost of sales or distribution) and lists the costs by type of expenditure. Shorn of all the incidentals, such a profit and loss account may look as in Table 5.4. Indeed, the main profit and loss account frequently shows only a total figure for 'operating costs', leaving the breakdown between raw materials, employment costs, etc. to the notes.

To give an example of 'the information shortfall', Table 5.5 shows extracts from British Steel's consolidated profit and loss accounts

Table 5.4 Profit and loss format 2

Turnover		100
Raw materials	30	
Other external charges	20	
Employment costs	25	
Depreciation	10	
Interest paid	3	
Pre-tax profit		12

Table 5.5 British Steel profit & loss account

£m	1996	1997
Turnover	7048	7224
Operating Costs	−6107	−6848
Trading Profit	941	376

Table 5.6 British Steel: accounts note 2

£m	1996	1997
Raw materials and consumables	2711	2967
Maintenance costs	521	573
Other external charges	952	1031
Employment costs	1331	1465
Depreciation	281	298
Grants released	−12	−10
Other operating costs	319	459
Changes in stock and work in progress	10	66
Own work capitalised	−6	−1
Operating costs total	**6107**	**6848**

for the financial years 1996 and 1997. This confirms that, whatever functions the main profit and loss account may have, disclosing the economics of the business is not one of them; the profit and loss format reveals little about British Steel's sales patterns or its operating cost structure. Note 2 to the accounts contained further analysis of the operating costs (Table 5.6). We are also given the amount for 'selling, general and administration expenses' (£485m in 1997) which will equate to some of the overhead cost but it cuts across the main cost classification in note 2. So, what does note 2 tell us that is of practical use? Does it help in distinguishing between fixed and variable costs?

- Raw materials is self-explanatory and might initially be assumed to be variable; this would be true for the iron ore, less so for the coal used in the furnaces and even less so for the tools and spares that are included within consumables.
- Maintenance is partly variable and partly fixed; as was pointed out in the analysis of the cycle, some work can be postponed more easily than other, and financial well-being is not irrelevant to the decision.
- Other external charges could be anything; the accounts offer no guidance. However, British Steel's 20-F report (see below) states that they include 'fuels and utilities, hire charges and carriage costs'. These are likely to be a mixture of fixed and variable costs.
- Employment costs are harder to evaluate and much depends upon the time period. Overtime can be increased or reduced; additional staff can be taken on or natural wastage can reduce numbers employed. However, if there is a change in output in the short term, it is unlikely to be accompanied by a significant variation in labour costs.
- Depreciation is the easiest of the fixed charges to isolate, and the nearest to a permanent fixed charge – at least until the plant is written off.

In short, a breakdown of this type takes us a little way in identifying fixed and variable costs – economic concepts which are easy to understand but which are not an integral part of modern accounting systems.[34] The comments above are in no way meant to be critical of British Steel's accounts, which do provide a good

34 The relationship between fixed and variable costs is discussed in more detail under 'The dynamics of the cycle' in Chapter 6.

breakdown of sales by type of steel product and by industry usage, coupled with informative market information – including the company's market share; it is just an example of the problems involved in obtaining economic information from accounting data, even in a one product company.

We have dwelt on the accounts format because it is the source of the profits figures we are trying to forecast; as the accounts show a financial path from sales to profits, they would appear to provide a ready-made forecasting framework. It is therefore important to stress that the difficulty we have in constructing a simple financial model is that whatever information we do have on costs (and we can find out more than is in the statutory accounts), it does not always come in a fixed costs, variable costs format. The cost information is also related to the type of input – employment costs for instance, which may be part fixed and part variable and those proportions changing according to the perceived state of the economic cycle. Thus, at each line of costs, the forecaster would be forced into assessing how much of the input is fixed and how much variable. ▷**Just because a cost has no direct relationship to sales does not mean that it is fixed.** ◁   ▷◁

The balance sheet as an information source

We can now look at the balance sheet as a source of information. The profit and loss account is, of course, the framework of the forecast; we start with the sales and work through the costs to the answer, or the profit. The balance sheet is primarily used to assess the financial strength of a company. Although this is outside our remit, the balance sheet can also be used as a source of information in its own right; for instance, the nature and size of individual assets may give clues as to the balance of the business. As an

Table 5.7 British Sky Broadcasting Group 1995 Balance Sheet	
Assets	**£m**
Tangible assets	45.8
Investments	1.5
Stocks	189.4

example, British Sky Broadcasting Group has figures given in Table 5.7 on its balance sheet.

At first glance, this asset information gives little away but the notes to the accounts reveal that £187m of the stock relates to television programme rights, giving an immediate clue to the economics of the business (and contradicting the author's previous assumption that the main cost of a satellite broadcasting company would be the satellites). A smaller corporate example is provided by Evans Halshaw, a motor dealer selling new and used cars, with all the associated after sales services. It also has a contract hire business and the note relating to tangible fixed assets gives specific information not available elsewhere, namely the value of the hire fleet and the annual depreciation charge. This acts as a pointer for all businesses whose primary function is the ownership of assets rented, leased or hired to third parties – be they plant hire or investment property companies: the balance sheets will contain significant information about the structure of the business.

Other sources of information

If the statutory accounts have their limitations, where else might one go for more information? Remember once again what it is we are trying to find out:

- the relationship between fixed and variable costs;
- the relative importance of the main costs so that differential price movements can be measured;
- and underlying it all, an operational understanding of the company (or industry) so that any anticipated external occurrence can be placed in context.

There is no finite limit on sources of information but there are particular areas which will tend to be more productive than others, some being specific to the company, (or internal), others external. They include

from *the company:*

- non-statutory information in the annual report;
- the original prospectus;
- acquisition documents;
- publicity department;

- Companies House;
- overseas statutory information;

from *other sources*:

- competitor companies;
- specialist books;
- trade organisations;
- government reports;
- market research organisations;
- newspapers and trade journals;
- stockbrokers' reports;
- international sources

and *semi-privileged information*

- contact with the subject company.

From the company

- The *non-statutory content of the Annual Report* can vary tremendously in the quality of the information supplied. While rarely setting out the cost structure in a formal manner, valuable comments may be made over a period of years as directors seek to explain particular events. Under the 1967 Companies Act, companies are supposed to provide a break-down of turnover and profits among significantly different activities and geographical regions. The standard of *segmental reporting* improved considerably during the 1980s and is a valuable source of information on the balance of the activities within the company. Typically, the breakdown by activity is wholly independent of the breakdown by location. In other words, you can see what profit has been made from motor components, and what profit from the USA. What will not be clear is how much of the motor component profit is earned in the USA or, conversely, how much of the US profit is derived from motor components. Sometimes it is possible to construct a matrix that reconciles these alternate breakdowns.
- The *original prospectus* is produced to demanding standards and often contains information about the structure of the business, the location of assets, spread of customers, etc.,

which the directors then decide is far too sensitive to reproduce in subsequent annual reports. As the years distance the company from its prospectus, the value of the information loses its topicality but there are occasions where the prospectus can still provide an interesting insight into the company – particularly for someone looking at it for the first time.[35] Subsequent fund-raising documents (typically rights issues) may also serve the same purpose, albeit on a more modest scale.

- *Acquisition documents* give, for obvious reasons, considerable information about the company being acquired, to a level that is unlikely to be referred to again.
- *Publicity departments* often supply briefing documents to give a better understanding of the company. Company journals can be a good source of information on the start of new projects – new factories, joint ventures, overseas expansion. Sometimes companies produce reviews of their own industry or particular market segments and these can be found in the most unlikely places – the small quoted company, William Ransom, produces an authoritative review of the European herbal drinks market.
- *Subsidiary accounts:* to the extent that the company operates through separate subsidiary companies, which more closely approximate to the economic activities, analysis of these accounts (filed at Companies House) can provide additional information. For example, the accounts of Lombard North Central and Royscot Trust provide valuable information on the leasing activities of National Westminster Bank and Royal Bank of Scotland. This information will complement the segmental analysis referred to above, and will often provide additional levels of detail on operating costs. A very simple example follows.

Bryant is a leading UK housebuilder, with additional interests in construction. Notes to the group accounts quantified the turnover and operating profit coming from each of these activities. However, the housing division traded through four separate subsidiaries, three regional and one functional. Table 5.8 shows the turnover, operating profit and profit margins for each of these subsidiaries. The comparison of the total with the divisional figure for housing given in the group accounts is to

---

35 Copies of old prospectuses can be found in the annual volumes of *Extel Book of Prospectuses and New Issues*.

Table 5.8 Bryant housebuilding subsidiaries

Year to	Turnover (£m)			Operating profit (£m)		
	1993	1994	1995	1993	1994	1995
Central	101	132	168	19.7	25.1	26.1
Northern	18	45	69	0.9	5.5	7.2
Southern	105	121	120	(3.1)	4.6	11.4
Scotland	–	–	21			3.3
County Homes	5	22	(0.3)	(0.2)	(0.2)	–
Total	224	302	399	17.3	35.0	47.8
cf. Divisional Total in						
Accounts	*224*	*306*	*401*	*17.4*	*33.9*	*46.2*

Year to	Margins (%)		
	1993	1994	1995
Central	19.5	19.1	15.6
Northern	4.9	12.3	10.4
Southern	(2.9)	3.8	9.5
Scotland	–	–	15.8
County Homes	(4.9)	(0.8)	–
Total	7.7	11.6	11.8
cf. Divisional Total in			
Accounts	*7.8*	*11.1*	*11.8*

Note: Figures may be subject to rounding errors.

show that the researcher has, in fact, identified the substance of the business – there are no large unexplained discrepancies.

Bryant's traditional area of activity is the Midlands. Anyone who had looked at the subsidiaries' returns for 1993 (a difficult year for the industry) would have seen that the Central region – 45% of turnover – accounted for over 100% of the operating profit. Nowhere else was this information, crucial in understanding how the company made its profit, ever disclosed. The subsequent recovery in profit came from the under-performing regions, yet it can be seen that Bryant's heartland remained the area generating the best margin.

A word of warning should accompany any reference to the use of subsidiary accounts: inter-company transfer pricing, management charges and overhead allocation can distort the published figures.

- Related to the use of UK subsidiary company accounts is the fact that similar filing requirements exist in other countries – though in the author's experience, they can be remarkably difficult to track down. Also, UK companies that are listed in the US have to file *supplementary reports* with the Securities and Exchange Commission (SEC) (10-K and 20-F). The annual 10-K includes the management's analysis of the financial condition of the company and of the operational results; the analysis is usually far more detailed than in the published group accounts and does appear to be written as if the objective is to explain rather than to hide. New registrations of securities for listing will also file a report known as the 20-F.

There may also be overseas subsidiaries with local stock exchange quotation, thus providing the whole range of corporate information. For example, Cable & Wireless owns Hong Kong Telecommunications quoted, not surprisingly, in Hong Kong, and BICC has Metal Manufacturers quoted in Australia.

From other sources

- *Other companies* in the same industry may supply fuller, or even different, background information. One company may be particularly helpful with revenue details, another with costs.
- *Books* have been written on most large industries, particularly the traditional manufacturing industries and those that have a high public profile. These will describe the manufacturing processes and, in varying degrees, the economics of the industry. Examples include the Woodhead Publishing 'Equities' series which include Construction, Mining, Oil, Media and Pharmaceuticals but any trawl through a decent reference library will produce a multitude of others.
- *Trade organisations* are often surprisingly secretive about their members' activities but they can be a useful source of information, particularly if the forecaster has specific non-contentious questions.
- *Government reports* have been providing invaluable information for decades. The Monopolies Commission Reports have been the longest running and these always open with an effective analysis of the business before giving its conclusions. The industrial and corporate detail provided can far exceed material published elsewhere: the 1997 *Report on Domestic Electric Goods* ran to four volumes and over 2800 pages. An

Table 5.9 Revenue account of five leading exhibitors

Revenue	£m	Costs	£m
Box office takings	946	Film rental payments	342
Screen Advertising	56	Concession cost of sales	105
Concessions	281	Advertising and publicity	40
Other revenue	21	Staff	275
		Depreciation	101
		Other operating costs	260
Total	**1304**	**Total**	**1123**

Table 5.10 British Gypsum costs as % of sales

Cost analysis	(%)
Materials	28.4
Direct wages	8.3
Energy	8.4
Total direct costs	45.1
Works indirect expenses	19.8
Bought in for re-sale	4.6
Carriage	8.8
	78.3
Overheads	7.7
Profit before taxation	14.0

example of the cost and revenue breakdowns that can be obtained is taken from the recent report on the film industry (Table 5.9).

If one delves into the past, there have been other organisations that have taken a similar approach to presenting the evidence and these can still offer a valuable insight into the operating structure of a business. Plucking such a report at random from my own shelves, I offer the Price Commission's 1978 *Report on British Gypsum* (the main operating subsidiary of BPB Industries) which contained the breakdown of costs as per Table 5.10.

A more recent source of material has been the reports of the various regulatory authorities set up to regulate the privatised public utilities. A whole range of industries now have detailed annual reports surveying their progress and including useful historical material. For instance, OFTEL regulates the telecommunications industry and the annual report of the

Director General includes 10 year runs of price changes for British Telecom, across the full range of its call bands and a weighted average thrown in for good measure.

- Specialist *market research* organisations produce detailed reports although these may be for a restricted customer base and usually very expensive, e.g. Economist Intelligence Unit, Mintel, CSO-Taylor, Nelson AGB Partnership and KeyNote Publications. However, they can normally be accessed at the large reference libraries.
- *Press articles* on specific issues, especially in the trade press. In this context, access to computer services (e.g. Reuters' Textline) that can search for particular topics is a welcome short cut.
- *Stockbrokers' reports*, though these are normally only available to their clients, and the larger ones at that. One problem with this source is that you may actually be a stockbroker, so read on.
- *International sources* replicate those already listed but are included here as a reminder that sources need not be confined to the company's home country. For example, Boeing produces an excellent annual review of the airline industry which contains 20 year forecasts of air travel by region and aeroplane deliveries by type; this would be of relevance to any UK manufacturer of aircraft components.

Semi-privileged information

Profit forecasts for third parties, i.e. a company that does not employ the forecaster, can be made by anyone – other companies, private investors, stockbrokers and investment houses. In practice, the bulk of the regular and the detailed forecasts are prepared by investment houses and these firms employ teams of specialists whose full-time occupation is industry and company forecasting. These professional forecasters have access to one source of information not available to the true outsider – the company itself; this relationship is sufficiently important to merit separate discussion (see below). Stockbrokers, for instance (normally specialists in a particular industry), have the opportunity to attend presentations made after preliminary, and sometimes interim, results announcements and go on group visits to operating locations. Individual visits to members of the management team, usually the finance director, are common, as is telephone access.

Talking to the company – inside/outside information

The formal objective of a company visit is to understand the background to the current trading position and the corporate strategy so as to facilitate the preparation of 'independent' forecasts. However, over time the financial analyst will have the opportunity of amassing a wealth of background information. This becomes of particular relevance when unforeseen events occur, enabling the financial analyst to put them into perspective immediately and to make the appropriate changes to his forecasts. For instance, it normally matters little in the forecasting of a cement company's profits whether its kilns are fired by oil or coal. If, however, there is a disturbance to the oil market that creates a substantial difference in the relative cost of the two fuels, then that piece of information suddenly becomes relevant; the financial analyst would also want to know whether the company bought on the spot market or had long term supply contracts. This is the type of information that is acquired with time and experience, the possession of which enables the financial analyst to react more quickly and, hopefully, more accurately, to changes in the external environment.

The relationship between company and broker has changed over the years, not necessarily to the benefit of independent thought. A murky world grew up in the 1970s and 1980s in which the supposedly independent forecaster became ever closer to the managements of the companies whose profits were being forecast. The progressive tightening of insider trading definitions has threatened these cosy relationships, as has the realisation that, during the recession in the early 1990s, the supposed inside guidance from the companies often proved less than accurate; this raises the interesting question of whether companies themselves realise what is happening during periods of rapid change. Nevertheless, although best practice now frowns on finance directors giving explicit guidance to individual analysts on profits, the provision of all the background and supporting information necessary for the financial analyst to make a balanced judgement on profits is still encouraged. It is even suggested that the provision of guidance on profits has not wholly disappeared.

Most of the debate on the relationship between the financial analyst and the company has centred on the specific issue of the profits forecast. However, behind that lies the large scale provision of information to analysts, usually stockbrokers, but with an increasing proportion of investing institutions being represented in the information dissemination process. Such is the demand for information that large companies may even have specific investor relations officers, a practice long established in the USA. The justification for this 'service' is that if outsiders are going to write reports on the company then it is in the company's interests that the information contained in the reports bears some semblance to the truth. An incidental thought might be that voluntarily providing information gives its originators a greater degree of control over its content and, perish the thought, a generally helpful and co-operative attitude may even influence the share price recommendation.

Those forecasters outside the charmed circle may be intrigued to know what form this flow of information takes. Typically, the larger companies (virtually all the FT 250 index companies and more) will have two presentations a year for financial analysts, on the day of the announcement of the interim and final results. At the analysts' meetings:

- the senior management will give additional detail on the historic results, over and above that contained in the published statement – most companies provide hard copies of information shown on slides (I cannot see why any outsider should not ask for the same information);
- there will normally be some comment on current trading and future expectations;
- there will be an open question and answer session;
- and, most prized of all, there will probably be an opportunity to talk privately to individual directors (if only that irritating competitor would go back to his office!).

There may also be visits to site locations. The company might want to show off its new superstore format in Bradford, or give a presentation on the packaging division it bought last year in Scotland. As the larger companies have expanded overseas, so the analysts' trips to France, Germany and the US have multiplied, giving unrivalled opportunities not only to see the business on the ground, but to spend concentrated periods of time with management, be it on the factory floor or in the hotel bar. One friendly 'I think you are being a bit pessimistic, Fred'[36] can be every bit as good as a day's intensive model building.

Apart from the direct contacts, the financial analyst often can pick up the telephone at any time outside the close period[37] to check on information that may be topical. 'There is talk of international steel prices edging up – is it correct?' Or, 'what effect is the recent currency strength/weakness having on your export margins?'

Financial analysts will frequently write reports on companies and send in drafts for comment. For any substantive report, I would regard this as best practice for it is a rare report by an outsider that cannot be factually improved by a helpful insider. To the extent that the report has been prepared after a visit to the company then courtesy alone, though not the subject of this book, would argue for the submission of a draft. The exercise of correction frequently leads to additional information being provided and sometimes financial analysts may specifically indicate in their drafts areas where they would like additional information to complete their report. It is not unknown for analysts to put in provocative profits 'guesstimates', hoping to profit from that facet of human nature that delights in telling others that they are wrong, a ploy better suited to Stephen Potter's *Gamesmanship* and *Oneupmanship* books and easily recognised by a finance director and countered with a 'no comment'.

This might be the appropriate point to say that the forecaster, when being given any information, whether it be background factual material or guidance on the profits forecast itself, should always ask the question: why am I being given this information? It may be that your source is naturally helpful; it may be his job to answer questions; or he may prefer reports that are written about his company to be factually accurate. He may, however, wish to influence your attitude to the company, your presentation of the nature of its business and, indeed, the actual profits forecast itself.

---

36 Today's version is more likely to be 'I think you will find that you are below the consensus', to which the correct response might be 'Does this cause you concern?'
37 The two months immediately preceding the interim or full year profits declaration, or from the period end if shorter.

The forecaster's art also includes the ability to decide whether his source really knows what is happening. There was a reference above to the poor quality of the supposed inside guidance at the beginning of the 1990s. ▷**Many financial analysts are apt to blame the hand that feeds them when they get their forecasts wrong: 'The finance director misled me' is the plaintive cry. Perhaps they should remember that the finance directors are just as prone to being misled by their operational colleagues.**◁

6 The short term profits forecast

Summary

After a reminder that we are looking at our subject companies as outsiders, Chapter 6 opens by outlining the simple model most appropriate for forecasters who have neither full access to the business data, nor unlimited time. Throughout, there is an emphasis on simplicity with the model focusing only on those factors that are material. For any business, there are always two or three key influences on profits – get this input wrong and the most complicated model becomes irrelevant.

A worked example of a model for a hypothetical newspaper publishing company is given, followed by exercises in recognising cyclical profits patterns and their relationship with the industry cycle. After these simple exercises, we move on to a more detailed discussion of the dynamics of the profit cycle – whether companies can influence their own destiny, how managements react and, inevitably, why the past is not always a guide to the future. The main body of the chapter finishes by taking the reader through from trading profits to the proverbial bottom line.

The chapter concludes with a section called 'Forecasting the unexpected', an apparent contradiction in terms. Nevertheless, there are useful pointers to what style of management and what kind of conditions can suggest that the unexpected is more likely to happen with some companies than with others.

The outsider's approach

By now, we should be familiar with the forces that influence both long term growth and cyclical movements in demand. We know that constraints of time and resources make it critically important for us to be able to recognise 'patterns' of economic and industrial behaviour. It may be that we are trying to short cut the forecasting process to produce a response that is required immediately. Hopefully, more time is available to the forecaster and he is using his familiarity with the patterns to direct his resources to the most commercially sensitive areas of the forecast – is this a turning point I see before me? Is this growth product reaching maturity? Even if we are doing no more than using someone else's forecast and need to assess its likely validity, the ability to recognise the economic patterns remains an important tool.

Chapter 4, Market share, provided the bridge between the industry forecast and the company profits forecast. It is a commonplace that not all companies in the same sector 'perform' in identical fashion and we have seen that this differential performance can be very substantial – and happen within a surprisingly short space of time. The combination of the industry forecast and the assessment of market share will take the forecaster through to company sales, the starting point (in theory though not always in practice) of the corporate profits forecast.[38] We must now examine the process by which the forecaster moves from sales to profits and, in doing so, will continue to stress one of the central themes of the book – the importance of pattern recognition.

The translation of a forecast of volume sales into a forecast of profits encompasses a complex relationship between selling prices, input costs, capacity utilisation and the proportions of fixed and variable costs; moreover, these relationships may vary according to the time horizon. In the ideal world the forecaster would have a model of the company's cost structure and could therefore apply his forecast assumptions through from the top line to the bottom line. It is at this point that we realise the principal difference between the insider, i.e. the corporate executive, and the outsider with little access to the information that a sensible person might consider essential for the preparation of a meaningful forecast.

38 In the days of full and frank communication between the quoted company and the financial analyst, it was not unknown for the latter to start with the profits forecast and work out what his assumptions needed to be.

We will look at the outsider's problems in two ways:

- how to obtain the cost structure and pricing detail – *the information shortfall*; and
- how to short circuit the whole process – *pattern recognition*.

Should the reader think that, as an outsider, he is on a hiding to nothing in making a forecast of somebody else's business, the author's personal observation is that ▷**possession of detailed management information does not necessarily make that management's judgements of the future any better.**◁ It is not impossible for managements to become bogged down in the wealth of detail that they possess, when rebudgeting can take weeks, and next year is generally assumed to be the same as this year, only a little bit better. I have never ceased to be surprised at the special pleading used by managements at the onset of each recession to show why 'This time it will be different'. It never is. Managements frequently underestimate the volume downturn that they will face – refer back to the fallacy of the non-cyclical business. Similarly, managements rarely anticipate the full extent of price cutting. How many times has one heard 'There are only a limited number of major firms in the … market: it makes no sense for any of us to start cutting prices'. Whatever the main board may want, there is always someone at an operational level looking to protect production levels with some judicious 'flexibility'. If the insider has the advantage of access to the detailed information, he has the disadvantage of standing too close. In contrast, the outsider has a greater flexibility, a wider range of forecasting experience to draw on and, most important, a healthy degree of cynicism.

Model building

Keep it simple

We return now to model building, with the hope that the warnings delivered in Chapter 1 have been remembered – beware model building as a substitute for thinking. If you want to explore financial modelling in detail, Neil Hogg's *Business Forecasting*

Using Financial Models[39] provides a comprehensive view. Unlike our standpoint, Hogg implicitly assumes that the reader is an 'insider' (i.e. part of the company management or an adviser) and therefore uses more detailed corporate data than will be accessible to the 'outsider'. But even he has some excellent warnings on the pitfalls of financial modelling especially when using spread sheet analysis. In the Introduction, Hogg distinguishes between financial modelling by the 'pragmatist' and the 'theorist':[40]

- The pragmatist 'keeps the model computationally simple and focuses on carrying out the arithmetic that might previously have taken place on large sheets of analysis paper. The model is, therefore, a means of presenting a body of input data in a commonly understandable format and allowing straight-forward manipulation of these results. However, that is not to say that these models cannot be both large and complicated'.
- The theorist 'makes greater use of relationships built into the model itself to give explanatory power to the modelling process, as opposed to using the profits model as a prompt, as in the Pragmatist's Approach'.

Our approach clearly falls into the pragmatist's camp but, even so, we are still coming at the task from a different direction from Hogg. The financial models that we are discussing are so far removed from the complexity of the insiders' models that one almost searches for a less pretentious expression. ▷ **The outsider should start by admitting to his own ignorance and to his limitations. To represent the reality of what he knows, or is capable of knowing, the first essential of the model is that it should be as simple a structure as possible. While this is an approach that may be born of necessity, it does lead the forecaster to focus attention on the materiality of the model.** ◁ The model should only attempt to isolate those influences on profits that are both:

- significantly different from each other, and
- of significance to the total.

All too often, forecasts contain line after line of individual costs, all of which are assumed to increase by exactly the same percentage;

39 Pitman, London, 1994.
40 A similar distinction is made between 'subjective' and 'model-based' forecasts in Holden, Peel and Thompson *Economic Forecasting: an Introduction*, Cambridge, 1990.

they add nothing to the forecasting process, waste the preparer's time and make it hard for the user to focus on the key factors in the forecast. Equally, the inclusion of a line for postage, on the grounds that first class stamps have increased in price, fails on the test of materiality.

The first stage in moving from a volume sales forecast to a profits forecast is to assess the impact of operational gearing. If all expenditure is totally variable, then a 10% change in volume would produce a 10% change in profits; that it does not, reflects the existence of fixed costs. In practice, the outsider may find it difficult to do more than approximately estimate the company's fixed costs and variable costs. If he can, the simple model for a one product business would look as per Table 6.1 with the forecaster applying his volume assumptions as appropriate.

In this most basic of models, the forecaster is simply illustrating the gearing effect of fixed costs for a given increase in demand. There is no price change assumed which is often a convenient first approach, allowing the volume changes to be assessed in isolation. Using the historic figures in Table 6.1, Graph 6.1 shows how profits would vary with changes in either volume or the fixed cost ratio. Thus, Graph 6.1(a) illustrates the accelerating rise in profits as volume growth increase; similarly, Graph 6.1(b) shows the change in profits derived from a constant 5% increase in volume but at different levels of fixed costs. It will be observed that profit is a residual, although we discuss later the extent to which changes in the 'residual' feed back to items 'above the line'.

It is important to recognise the relative degree of exposure that some companies have to volume gearing. For continuous process

Table 6.1 Simple company model

	Historic	Change in volume (%)	Outcome	Change (%)	
Sales	100.0	+10	110.0	10.0	⎫
Fixed costs	30.0	–	30.0	–	Operational
Variable costs	60.0	+10	66.0	10.0	gearing
Total costs	90.0		96.0	6.7	⎭
Trading profit	10.0		14.0	40.0	⎫
Interest paid	3.0		3.0		Financial
Pre-tax profit	7.0		11.0	57.1	gearing

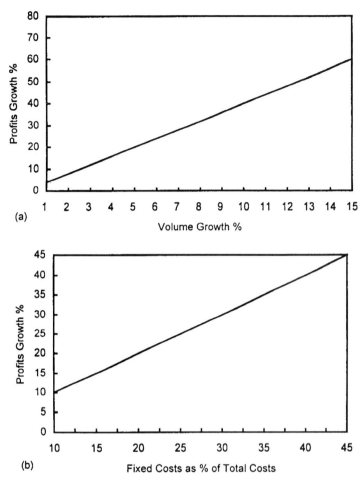

Graph 6.1 (a) Volume gearing 30% – the accelerating rise in profits across a range of volume assumptions; (b) Volume growth 5% – the change in profits derived from a constant 5% increase in volume but at different levels of fixed costs.

companies such as British Steel or Pilkington (glass), there is a very limited ability in the short term to turn volumes off – the effect of a fall in demand comes straight through to the bottom line. Similarly, there are businesses where output can easily be controlled, such as mining, but where the price change comes straight through to profits.

From the simple model in Table 6.1, one can then begin to

Table 6.2 Simple model – addition of pricing

	Historic	Change in Volume	Change in Price	Outcome	Change (%)
Sales	100.0	+10	+6	116.6	16.6
Fixed costs	30.0		+5	31.5	5.0
Variable costs	60.0	+10	+5	69.3	15.5
Total costs	90.0			100.8	12.0
Trading profit	**10.0**			**15.8**	**58.0**
Interest paid	3.0			3.0	
Pre-tax profit	**7.0**			**12.8**	**82.9**

introduce additional factors, the most obvious being price assumptions – relating both to sales and costs. Table 6.2 takes the volume assumptions and fixed cost structure as in Table 6.1 and suggests a 5% increase in input prices and, just to be different, a slightly higher rate of selling price increases.

Even at this stage, the forecaster can be questioning the answer – an integral part of the forecasting process. Does an 83% increase in pre-tax profits seem surprising? Would a company enjoying that degree of profits growth be pushing through price increases? Would cost inflation be higher? Is there sufficient spare capacity to permit 10% growth without any increase in the quantum of fixed costs? Is this the stage in the cycle when we normally see very rapid profits growth?

The next stage is that the forecaster can begin to fine tune the model to allow different assumptions if revenue is derived from more than one source; and to determine whether the company has any important input costs that might experience price movements significantly different from the general rate of inflation, or from the assumed rate of sales price inflation.

Looking at sales, we could take a newspaper company as an example; in that case the two revenue streams would be the obvious ones of the volume of copies sold multiplied by the net selling price, plus the advertising volumes times the advertisement rates. If one is looking at a food retailer, then estimates of the rate of food sales growth and food price inflation will be sufficient. If it is an expanding company then there could be an additional line that distinguishes between new stores and the growth in the existing business.

On costs, we could keep with our newspaper publisher where we would want to isolate the price of paper; for a housebuilder it would be the price of land. A cost breakdown which shows only newsprint and 'other costs' is not revealing the forecaster's ignorance of the structure of the business – in contrast, it shows an ability to isolate and focus only on that which has a material impact on the forecast. The slightly enlarged model would be constructed as per Table 6.3. For the newspaper company, revenue streams 1 and 2 would be circulation and advertising and the key raw material would be paper.

It is, of course, possible to construct profits models considerably more complicated than this and the author might well have appeared more impressive had he done so. However, there is a place for honesty and it must be stressed that ▷**when complicated models are drawn up by outsiders, they serve little purpose other than to bamboozle the reader; even worse, their spurious accuracy often appears to fool the very person who has prepared the forecast. The information necessary for the detailed model is rarely available to the outsider. Where the detail is available, the additional items tend to be less significant and they will be swamped by any errors in the assumptions made for those items that appeared in the simple forecast. Even worse, fiddling about with the minor elements of a forecast can produce a false sense of comfort and take the forecaster's eye off those assumptions that are really material.**◁

Thus, to stick to the earlier examples, if you are looking at a newspaper business, and get the assumptions about circulation

Table 6.3 Profits model – addition of variables

		Change in		Outcome	Change (%)
		Volume	Price		
Revenue stream 1	60.0	+10	+8	71.3	18.8
Revenue stream 2	40.0	+5	+5	44.1	10.3
Sales	100.0	+8		115.4	15.4
Fixed costs	30.0		+5	31.5	5.0
Key raw material	25.0	+8	+12	30.2	
Other variable costs	35.0	+8	+5	39.7	13.4
Total costs	90.0			101.4	12.7
Trading profit	**10.0**			**14.0**	40.0
Interest paid	3.0			3.0	
Pre-tax profit	**7.0**			**11.0**	**57.1**

and cover price, advertising sales and paper costs even broadly right, it is difficult to imagine the need to worry about the rest. And for the housebuilder the key factors would be housing activity and house prices for revenue and land prices within costs. Putting it round the other way, if the forecaster was to get those three elements wrong then the totality of the forecast would be beyond saving, however many lines it had. The reader can try working out the 'key determinants' for his own favourite industries.

A worked example

Having looked at the sources of information available to us, both in the company accounts and elsewhere, let us take an industry example and see how far we can progress as outsiders in constructing a working model – in this case, we will look once again at our hypothetical newspaper company.

As mentioned above, the newspaper industry obtains its income from two clearly identifiable sources – the cover price of the paper itself, and the sale of advertising space. It would be hard to find a better documented source of sales than for newspapers, as the Audit Bureau of Circulations certifies and publishes sales figures for every publication each month. The selling price is, of course, on full public view (though newsagents' discounts may not be). Trends in advertising revenue (with forecasts) are published by NTC Publications in its *The Advertising Forecast*. Although the data are not journal-specific, the figures are broken down as far as quality nationals, etc.[41] On the costs side, one would need no specialist knowledge to work out that the main costs are newsprint, printing (which may or may not be in house), and editorial and production staff.

Four sets of accounts have been taken to see how much information is available. The mix of business differs, with The Telegraph plc being to all intents a one product business at the operating level with its eponymous weekly and Sunday titles. The others, Daily Mail & General Trust, Mirror Group and United Newspapers[42] have a greater range of newspaper titles,

41 It is possible to obtain information on individual newspapers' advertising from *ACNielsen-Meal* but only on request and at a negotiated cost.
42 Now United News and Media plc.

periodicals and other media interests. Nevertheless, when comparative data are available, the ratios are not that dissimilar. Thus, the Mirror Group and The Telegraph plc both disclose,[43] advertising/circulation splits that are 61/39% and 53/47% while United Newspapers states that advertising is 54% of turnover. Thus, for a newspaper publishing group that gave no information, a 55/45 turnover split in favour of advertising would not look to be a bad guess, and it could be fine tuned by seeing whether the mix of titles approximated more to The Telegraph plc or Mirror Group pattern.

On the cost side, the four sets of accounts produce the percentages shown in Table 6.4. None of these shows paper costs but information is around if you are looking for it. When Trinity International (a publisher of local newspapers) announced its 1994 results in March 1995, the *Financial Times* stated that newsprint accounted for about 12% of the company's costs. United Newspapers, however, reported with its 1994 results that newsprint accounted for 23% of its 'operating costs'. In 1995, The Telegraph plc actually quantified its newsprint bill at £55m against £43m in 1994.

Taking a line through the information above, extracted from the accounts, we could adapt the model shown in Table 6.3 to produce a pro-forma model for a newspaper publishing firm (Table 6.5).

Table 6.4 Publishing cost analysis

	Turnover	Operating profit	Total costs	Staff costs
Daily Mail	100	12	88	27
Mirror Group	100	24	76	22
The Telegraph plc	100	17	83	17
United Newspapers	100	14	86	29
Average	*100*	*17*	*83*	*24*

	Depreciation, hire and lease	Other costs	Of which raw materials
Daily Mail	6	55	18
Mirror Group	6	48	N/A
The Telegraph plc	4	62	N/A
United Newspapers	6	51	20
Average	*5*	*54*	*19*

43 1993 and 1994 accounts.

Table 6.5 Publishing model

	Historic	Change in Volume	Change in Price	Forecast	Change (%)
Advertising	55				
Circulation	45				
Sales		100			
Labour	24				
Depreciation	5				
Paper	12				
Other costs	42				
Total costs		83			
Trading Profit	**17**				

The model could be used to fine tune any of the companies above, or any other newspaper company for that matter, substituting the actual figures where available and the approximations for non-disclosed items. The Telegraph plc, for example, discloses advertising and circulation revenues but has an 'other costs' item that encompasses three-quarters of total costs.

Taking another of the information sources that we discussed earlier, the Monopolies Commission reports, in this case *The supply of national newspapers*:[44] 'With regard to direct publishing costs, editorial and pre-press facilities and printing plant represent major elements of fixed capital cost (in the short to medium term) and give rise to significant economies of production. ... Newsprint is the main component of variable cost and ... it accounts for some 75 to 85 per cent of incremental costs of production.' Unfortunately, the Report did not give the breakdown between total fixed and variable costs.

This has not been intended as a definitive exercise in model building for newspaper publishing; it has deliberately been prepared without guidance from the companies themselves or specialist analysts. This example has merely sought to indicate where the outsider might start: the data available in published accounts and their limitations; and alternative sources of information. The large reference libraries are full of specialist industry reports and studies and the diligent researcher will inevitably find much additional information – before he even puts a direct question to the company.

44 Cm 2438 December 1993, Para 3.14.

How the cycle works

The pattern of the cycle

Almost the opening paragraph in this book, repeated again at the start of this chapter, discussed the importance of pattern recognition. The question was posed – 'how is it that analysts … are able to produce almost instantaneous forecasts without having first gone through all the due processes?' The response was, of course, by drawing on their experience based on an ability to recognise a wide range of patterns of economic and corporate behaviour. Amongst the 'portfolio of patterns in his mental filing cabinet' will be those that crudely relate a company's profits to an industry statistic. The author again stresses that this is not meant to obviate detailed forecasting studies but pattern recognition does provide the rationale that underpins:

- the instant profits forecast that is a commonplace in the investment community;
- the self-checking that experienced forecasters will use when questioning each stage of the forecasting process;
- the checking mechanism whereby users of forecasts quickly decide whether the material before them is credible.

There follow three examples where profits cycles can be compared with an industry cycle, displaying recognisable patterns of behaviour. The first is taken from the motor industry, shown in Graph 6.2. In the top graph, trading profits of motor distributor Perry Group are plotted against the absolute level of new car registrations. The relationship is very close with the possible exception of the early 1980s; however, the lower graph shows Perry Group's profits compared with Ford registrations (Perry Group's main marque at that time) and the relative flatness in profits in the early 1980s has its counterpart in the Ford registrations.

The second example (Graph 6.3) is provided by the engineering company, Renold, whose profits have been plotted against engineering orders. It can be seen in the top graph that there is a close similarity between the pattern of percentage changes in new orders and the level of Renold's profits but that the relationship is lagged. By moving the new orders back one year in the lower graph, an almost perfect fit is produced.

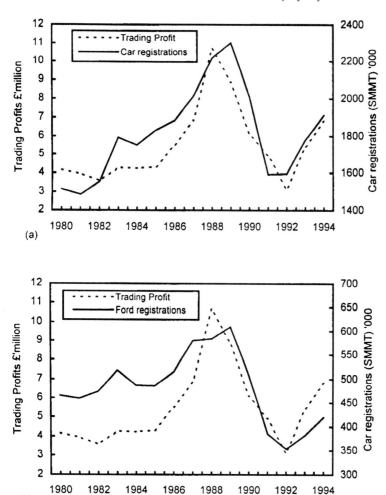

Graph 6.2 Perry Group profits: (a) against total car registrations; (b) against Ford registrations.

Finally, we look at Baggeridge Brick. In Graph 6.4 we see that the simple relationship between profits and an industry statistic is not especially helpful. This is because the growth in the scale of the business combined with the cumulative effect of inflation means that the earlier profits are very small in relation to those of more recent years. This demonstrates that there are no hard and fast rules about the way in which the industry statistic is used; the idea is to find the relationship that works best. Pattern recognition has been a theme of this book and preparing graphs of company

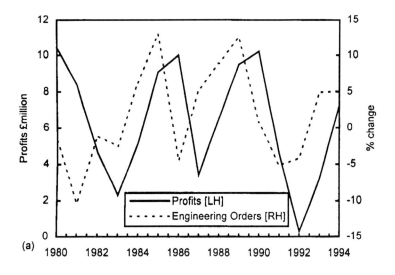

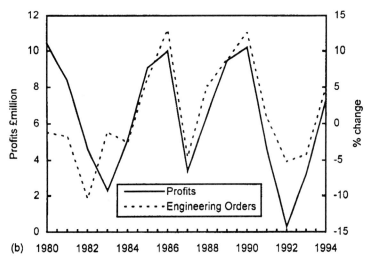

Graph 6.3 Renold profits: (a) against engineering orders; (b) against engineering orders lagged one year.

profits and industry statistics is often the first guide to the nature of the relationship or, indeed, in answering the question, is there a pattern? The Baggeridge example shows that one has to work at it.

A better fit between the industry statistics and profits is shown in Graph 6.5. Here we show the percentage change in Baggeridge Brick profits (rather than the absolute level) plotted (a) against the

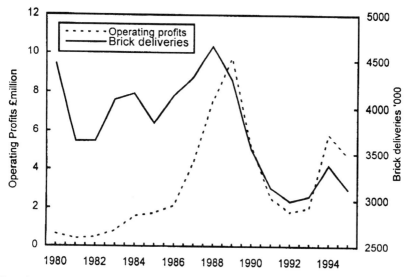

Graph 6.4 Baggeridge Brick profits.

absolute level of brick deliveries and (b) against the percentage change in brick deliveries.

The objective of this last section has been to illustrate the course of a typical cycle with examples showing the pattern and amplitude of profit movements in relation to an industrial cycle. Reliance by the forecaster on these patterns, on these relationships between an industry statistic and the individual company's profits, is based on an underlying logic. We start by stressing that it is essential for the forecaster to understand the dynamics of the industrial cycle and the way it impacts on the companies' profitability. Nevertheless, the forecaster recognises that he is an outsider and that for most companies the makeup of the revenue stream and the underlying cost structure is too complicated for him to reconstruct accurately. Even if the impact on profits of a given change in industry sales can be crudely approximated, this static representation of corporate activity will be quickly outdated by management response. However, past observation may have shown that, for instance, an $X\%$ change in industry sales, at a particular stage in the cycle, tends to lead to a $Y\%$ change in corporate profits. This is the 'experience' that forecasters draw on when making what appear to be instantaneous changes to their profits forecasts when external circumstances change.

141

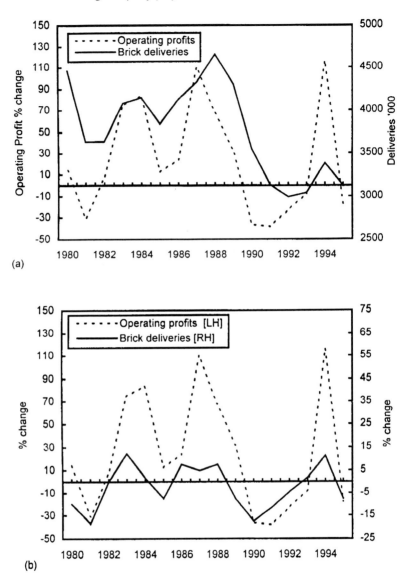

Graph 6.5 Baggeridge Brick profits: (a) *v.* absolute level of brick deliveries; (b) *v.* % change in brick deliveries.

The dynamics of the cycle

It may now be appropriate to return to the earlier comments about adapting the simple model. We have referred to improving our knowledge of the cost structure but the analysis goes deeper than that. Profit cycles have their own dynamics and the following description of the nature of the profits cycle was given in my book *Construction Equities: Evaluation and Trading*:[45]

> It is an unusual industry in which company profits do not respond, to a greater or lesser magnitude, to a sustained rise or fall in demand. In a manufacturing organisation, rising demand leads to greater capacity utilisation and hence lower unit costs; at the same time, that rising demand will also lead to price increases (whether direct or through a reduction in previous discounts). The magnitude of the profit increase created by the double effect of capacity utilisation and pricing will depend on the ability and willingness of the companies to exploit their advantages, and their perceived balance between short term gains and long term strategy. It may be argued that a monopolistic structure maximises the profit gain but, on the other hand, the fewer companies involved, the more likely they are to be able to exercise a responsible long term pricing policy.
>
> Depending on the capacity structure of the particular industry, the duration of the upturn, and the investment policy, the companies will eventually run into supply constraints of one form or another which push their costs up faster than selling prices, a reflection of suppliers, be they labour or materials, seeking their share of the excess profit. Seeing the shortage of capacity and the high returns, some producers will invest in new capacity with an unerring instinct for doing so as their industry reaches the top of its cycle.
>
> The downwards phase of the profits cycle is more or less a mirror image of the above with falling capacity utilisation and price competition. Eventually capacity is closed either voluntarily or through financial pressure.

▷ **One of the problems with models is that there is a tendency to suppose that the answers are fixed,**◁ that a given rise in volumes has the same effect on profits at all stages of the cycle. Furthermore, if the result of feeding in changes in output and costs is a 40% fall in profits, the model assumes that the management sits there and does nothing in response. The answer produced by the model may be perfectly valid in the short term but, for instance, an adverse movement in profits will very quickly bring forward corrective action on the part of the management, the most

---

45 Woodhead Publishing, Cambridge, 1994.

common being the shedding of peripheral costs and reduction in numbers employed, specifically designed to turn what was originally a fixed cost into a variable cost. Indeed, if the management has any competence, it too will be going through the same forecasting procedures as the outsider and will be trying to adapt its cost structure as demand falls and not after the event.

▷ **Thus, the forecaster should use the profits model first to see how a given change in demand would impact on profits – if nobody does anything about it. The second stage is a judgement on corporate reaction: how quickly will the management of the company and its competitors take remedial action?** ◁

We referred earlier to profits being a residual item. Mathematically that is true but the short term changes in that residual lead in turn to decisions to change (or attempt to change) the determining inputs, thereby altering the residual.

Not every company possesses the same ability to react to changed external circumstances: therefore, the forecaster must ask ▷ **whether the company has the ability to determine its own destiny.** ◁ One might distinguish between producers operating in monopolistic conditions and those in more perfectly competitive markets. The former will find it easier to alter the cost structure of the whole industry than will the latter. However, even in a competitive market, if all producers of a product are being affected in like manner, however many there are of them, they will be more likely to act in collective self-interest, parodying the action of a monopolist, than if the producers have different cost structures or operate in different environments.

Let us suppose that there are three producers of product A and the price of their principal raw material increases by 20%. We explore three alternative scenarios where, in each case, a profits model suggests a sharp fall in profits. So what?

1. If there is little possibility of substitution of product A, the producers will simply raise their prices to compensate for the raw material costs and profits return to where they were. Indeed, the price response may be so immediate that the theoretical answer produced by the model never happens even momentarily.[46]

46 It might be asked why, if the producers had the market power to increase their selling price, had they not been maximising their profits? Because they did not wish new entrants to the market to be attracted by an abnormally high return on capital.

144

2. Now suppose that there is the possibility of substitution for product A and its price can only be partially increased. Then the answer first produced by the model will be more realistic and the forecaster will feed in his raw material price increase and expect only limited selling price compensation.

3. The final scenario for our three producers of product A is if they have two different production processes, one based on raw material B and the other two using raw material C (akin to the earlier coal or oil example in the cement industry). If it is only raw material B that increases by 20% and C is unchanged then the ability of the affected producer to increase his prices will be minimal – probably dependent on the slack in the market and his competitors' production flexibility.

While stressing the importance of quantifying the external influences on sales and costs so that some estimate may be made of the resultant impact on profits, the exercise cannot be left there; you must also estimate the extent to which the companies can react. If the negative influences are experienced by all competitors, the easier the adjustments will be to make; if they have a selective impact on one company or group of companies then there may be little ability to secure compensatory adjustments. A common example of the latter is, of course, competition from imports where foreign producers may develop cost structures radically different from the domestic producers and some industries have totally failed to compensate.

This is a key forecasting lesson. Companies with a common interest have the capacity to get their act together. It may take a varying amount of time for 'common sense' to prevail but excess capacity can be taken out of, or allowed to drain from, an industry; prices can be edged up with the tacit agreement of the participants. The question becomes:

- Am I forecasting for a company operating in an industry where the cycle can run its natural course and where the profit recovery mechanisms can be expected to work? If so, is the structure of the industry one that will allow speedy rationalisation and response or is the return to a profit equilibrium likely to be long drawn out?
- Alternatively, is my company competing against other businesses which, by virtue of their location, ownership or production processes, are able to conduct their business in a

way that offers little opportunity to the natural processes of cyclical recovery?

We started this section by asking whether the company had the capacity to determine its own destiny; in effect, this involves making a judgement on the structure and nature of the industry in which the company operates. (This is particularly important for international businesses where the production costs and sales revenues may be in different countries with the consequent currency matching requirements.) However, the question implicitly assumes that, given the industry context, the management will go on to make the correct decisions out of a range of options that are open to it on pricing, costs and capacity. The other question that must therefore be raised, though it is more difficult to model, is: to what extent the management does actually have the ability to react in the best way? Or, as a colleague once put it to me – never underestimate the ability of management to screw it up. To assess this, we really need to go back to Chapter 4 where we discussed management's ability to determine market share.

The past is not always a guide to the future

Implicit in this approach is the assumption that cyclical behaviour patterns remain similar which, for the most part, they do. Nevertheless, the forecaster, having established the cyclical framework that he thinks is repeating itself, must then look to see if there are circumstances that are different from previous cycles. Is the magnitude of the cycle of a different order? Are there additional competitors who might react differently? Has the regulatory background changed, and so on? Think imaginatively!

The recession that ended the 1980s boom provides (because of its severity) a general example of a profits cycle which, for many industries, was different from its predecessors and forecasters who did not appreciate this had problems. Moving to the specific, the recent experience of the newspaper industry provides an example of an industry where the past would suddenly have stopped being a good guide to the future. The Telegraph plc's directors' report for 1993 provided useful statistical material, including a five year run of turnover, split between circulation and advertising (Table 6.6)

£m	1989	1990	1991	1992	1993
Table 6.6 The Telegraph plc					
Circulation	78	83	98	110	117
Advertising	153	136	118	123	133
Miscellaneous	3	3	3	4	6
Total turnover	234	222	219	237	256
Operating profit	*43.5*	*33.3*	*32.6*	*37.5*	*42.9*

clearly showing the cyclical nature of newspaper advertising, which we also remember from our earlier examples. This cyclicality is mirrored in the profits record, particularly in the first year of the recession. (A similar pattern emerges from the profits records of the other newspaper publishing companies discussed earlier.)

On the basis of a continued recovery in economic activity and, hence, advertising revenue, past relationships would have suggested a continued, and relatively strong, recovery in newspaper profits. In the event, The Telegraph plc's advertising revenue increased by 15% in 1994 but operating profits more than halved from £42.9m to £20.1m. Two things had happened: the price war in the national newspaper market, followed by a substantial increase in the price of newsprint. Could the break in the relationship between advertising revenue and profits have been anticipated? Hindsight is a useful forecasting tool but all that can reasonably be said about the price war was that the high returns on capital employed[47] provided the conditions wherein individual businesses might go for market share – particularly in an industry where the proprietors are known for taking strong positions. As for the newsprint cost increases, they could more easily have been anticipated: trade magazines would have indicated the surge of demand from the Far East; in any case, the newsprint industry is notoriously cyclical (see Graph 6.6) and no prolonged period of low newsprint prices could have been expected to continue.

While the newspaper price war was still raging, was there an objective way in which a forecaster might assess when the price cutting could end? The first response, as in so many other

47 If The Telegraph plc's operating profits for 1993 are compared with the operating assets less the intangible value attributed to the newspaper titles, then the return on capital can be seen to be exceptionally high.

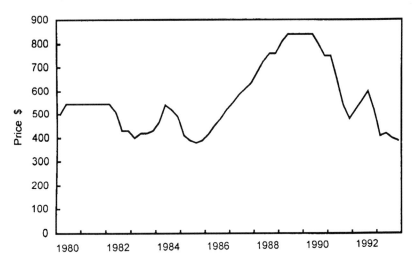

Graph 6.6 Pulp prices.

situations, is to ask 'what is normal?' or perhaps better, 'what is realistic?' Did a 48p cover price for the *Daily Telegraph* promise an abnormal return in which case it would have been unrealistic to look for a return to those price levels? (In the same way, it would be unrealistic to look for a return to the profit margins being earned by housebuilders in the boom of the late 1980s.) If the returns earned by national newspapers fall below 'acceptable' levels then there is an argument for forecasting an end to the price war. Of course, determining what are 'acceptable' returns is an art unto itself and price wars can often become matters of personal and corporate pride – sometimes it can take a new management to turn its back on the ways of the old.

Capital structure and the profits cycle

The relationship between variable and fixed costs is well understood in theory with, other things being equal, companies with high fixed costs being the most sensitive to changes in output – continuous process manufacturing with large economies of scale (and therefore a few large plants) usually provide the examples. Yet there are times when capital-intensive businesses can have a surprising degree of flexibility. Expansion and new capital investment often leaves behind an array of smaller plants, uneconomic in normal market conditions. When these high cost units are operated in boom conditions to meet what is perceived as a temporary upsurge in demand, they can be taken out of commission when demand falls with little impact on profitability.

Thus, as the cyclical downturn begins, management may appear relaxed about the profits implications knowing that, among other things, it has a degree of operating flexibility. However, if the recession deepens, that high cost capacity is all closed and the crunch comes as demand falls below the full capacity working of what one might call the base load plant. This is the point at which the profits suddenly appear to deteriorate. It is a phenomenon that often leads to companies signalling, perhaps to the surprise of outside forecasters, that they can cope with the recession – profits can be maintained. But, when the fall in volumes turns out to be greater than expected, profits are suddenly hit just at the point when outside forecasters have finally accepted the company's assertion that profits can be protected – the sucker punch.

We can continue with this scenario of a gradually deepening recession. As demand continues to fall, capacity working declines further and the pressure on profits is accentuated. If, say, there are five base load plants of equal size, the point eventually comes (at 80% utilisation) when one of those plants can be closed. The company returns to 100% capacity utilisation and operating profitability (ignoring pricing policy for the moment) is back to normal, albeit on a reduced volume of sales. Any number of variations on this theme are possible, depending on the number of plants, associated distribution costs, and depth of the recession. It explains why, in capital intensive businesses, profits do not always fall as soon as demand; why there can be a sudden hit to profits just when the company had appeared to be coping with the recession; and why profits can suddenly recover in the middle of a recession, only to fall again, or not, as the case may be. ▷ **The forecaster has to understand these phenomena, particularly if he is to avoid being led astray by managements assuring him that 'we can cope with the recession' and if he is to spot the false dawn, or dead cat bounce as it is sometimes insensitively described.** ◁

As capacity tends to be removed towards the end of the cyclical downturn when, by definition, the decline in demand is slowing, capacity utilisation can actually increase before demand has begun to rise: there can, therefore, be the apparent paradox of profits improving ahead of the increase in demand.

As an example of the way in which profits can recover before the industry cycle, I have taken a company no longer with us, London Brick now part of Hanson. London Brick provides an excellent corporate illustration as it was a sizeable one product company, with a significant market share, operating in an industry that prepared monthly delivery statistics and published list prices.

Because profits are declared on a half yearly basis, the winter first half is normally smaller than the second half. Nevertheless, it can be seen in Graph 6.7 that the small fall in brick deliveries in 1979 led to a much sharper fall in profits. Indeed, the near 30% fall in brick deliveries in the early 1980s hardly had any greater effect on profits. The answer lies in the management's expectations at the time. The fall in demand in 1979 was unexpected and the reduction in volumes had an immediate effect. The substantial decline that followed in 1980 was more quickly accompanied by cost reduction measures and reductions in capacity to try to preserve capacity utilisation. Thus, in 1981, brick deliveries were still falling, though the graph shows that the rate of decline was decelerating. By then, London Brick was cutting back its capacity aggressively to meet the earlier reductions in demand; although the absolute level of

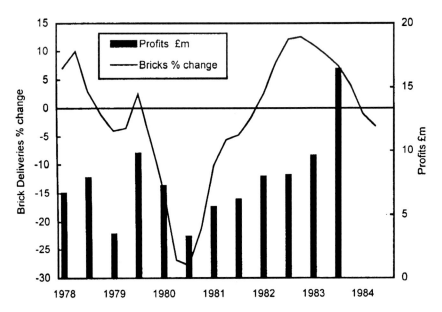

Graph 6.7 London Brick profits and the brick cycle.

brick sales continued to fall, they were now falling less rapidly than was capacity. At the bottom of the cycle, when the newspaper headlines were proclaiming a new low for brick deliveries, and brick stocks at a record high, London Brick was able to produce steady increases in profits. In 1984, Hanson bid for London Brick at what was clearly the top of the cycle; the defence document forecast doubled profits for the second half of 1983 with 1984 profits promised to be 'very good indeed'. Whatever else Hanson was able to do with a conservatively run company, the timing of the bid was interesting in the context of our cyclical analysis.

The parallel to the paradox of flexible fixed costs is the inflexibility of variable costs of which labour is the most important. As anyone with any employment experience, let alone management experience, already knows, employment levels are not turned on and off like a tap as volumes change. Indeed, to experience the fixed costs of labour, walk into any stockbroker's dealing room on a quiet day and look at the people sitting idly around. The expression 'people business' is used to describe firms, such as brokers or advertising agencies, where the main asset is the staff, who can leave at the theoretical moment's notice. That may be so, but when times are hard, they have an irritating habit of wanting their monthly pay cheque. Variable bonuses may alleviate the problem to some extent but labour remains a high fixed cost element. Natural wastage and recruitment freezes will help in the early stage of a downturn though all too often this means no more than there being insufficient secretaries to type the highly paid executives' work. Then comes the decision on redundancies. However, the long term interests of a 'people business' lie in keeping its teams of people, with all their experience and client contacts, together. This is felt all the more keenly if the only result of redundancies would be for those employees (with some of their better client relationships) to reappear in the employ of a competitor taking a longer term view. The practical reality of running a long term business may therefore be to sustain high fixed labour costs through periods of recession – or at least while the competition is doing so.

Manufacturing and service industries employing semi-skilled or unskilled labour may have a greater degree of operating flexibility with employees but there are high costs to a temporary reduction in numbers – redundancy payments, retraining, dislocation, morale and long term reputation. The cost of redundancies, the impact on morale and the managerial admission of defeat, can mean that the decision to cut staff numbers is left so late that it may almost immediately precede the cyclical recovery. Redundancy is not always instituted at the beginning of a cyclical downturn, managements preferring to wait until they are convinced that the downturn is for real – which can explain why some companies cut back at the bottom of the cycle. The operating characteristics of the particular business will also determine the level of labour flexibility, for instance, continuous processes with a predominantly supervisory staff, or small discrete operating teams (you cannot take 10% off a team of three).

▷ **The forecaster must recognise that the distinction between capital and labour may owe more to theory than to practical reality, that the two are interdependent. He must assess the total flexibility of the whole business: whether individual production units can be scaled down or closed in line with any given fall in demand; and the speed and cost of such response. A business may be described as capital intensive but if that capital can be varied in a smooth progression then it may prove far more recession-proof than a supposedly labour-intensive business.** ◁

Disparate businesses

The discussion of profits forecasting has presupposed a homogeneous corporate structure with the hope that there are also clearly identifiable volumes, selling prices and costs which can be modelled, however crudely. The reality is that few large businesses are centred around one dominant single business concept operating in the domestic market – they are not all Tescos. The privatised water and electricity companies provide a range of examples, although without lengthy track records as independent companies. In many cases where, at first glance, there appears to be a homogeneous business, there are other interests which cannot be analysed in the same way as the mainstream activity. Keeping to the retail industry, Sainsbury and Marks & Spencer in the UK provide examples of this problem as both companies gradually develop their overseas operations and non-traditional retailing outlets.

These examples have been deliberately chosen to be only

marginal deviations from the forecaster's ideal homogeneous company, yet already they pose procedural problems. Does the forecaster model build using the global costs available from the group accounts, thus lumping together businesses with substantially different characteristics and profitability; or does he work from the divisional analysis, accepting that the financial information is limited to turnover and operating profit? In practice, the forecaster will be taking views of the UK economy that are different from those of the US or French economy; views of the company's market strengths at home and overseas; and views of the UK food retailing and DIY markets. It seems inevitable that the forecaster will want to look at the businesses in terms of their different operating units. The profits model will still be a valid method of rationalising the thought process but it will be a profits model derived from a greater approximation than one based on the consolidated accounts.

Without resorting to the extreme of the industrial holding company or conglomerate, there are many companies that, even though they may appear to operate within one industry, actually contain a range of subsidiaries that have entirely different profit performance characteristics. A typical example would be the engineering company GKN which includes within its operations vehicle components for cars (the consumer cycle) and commercial vehicles (the capital goods cycle); defence (armoured vehicles and, most recently, Westland helicopters); industrial pallets; waste management; and vending machines, all with an international mix. Alternatively, one could instance Smiths Industries; its

Table 6.7 Smiths Industries' operating profits (£m)

	1996		1997	
By division				
Aerospace	45.3		59.3	
Medical systems	73.1		74.7	
Industrial	49.7		60.6	
Total		168.1		194.6
By geographic region				
UK	75.1		86.6	
USA	71.4		84.1	
Continental Europe	17.2		14.0	
Other	4.4		9.9	
Total		168.1		194.6

operating profits are shown in Table 6.7 for the period 1995/6–1996/7.

It was suggested earlier that the forecaster could parallel the model building exercise by comparing a company's profit record with the appropriate industry indicator. Examples of cyclical pattern recognition taken from the motor and engineering industries were shown in Graphs 6.2 to 6.5. Although this enables the forecaster to see at a glance the extent to which profits have fluctuated with the industry cycle, it is not always easy in practice to construct such historic relationships. Few companies stay the same shape; acquisitions can distort the profits record and it would be a lengthy exercise to go through old accounts (even when they can be obtained) to plot the underlying profits record.

For the larger concerns, particularly those with an international spread of business, the group profit and loss account may be less helpful as an indicator than the divisional analysis. Thus, in the Smiths Industries example, the forecaster would want to look separately at the main operating divisions. Here, we run into another common difficulty, in addition to that of acquisitions – the definitions may change from year to year. For instance, back in 1983, Smiths had seven listed divisions which only reduced to the present three in 1989. Even after that there have been years when exceptional items and property have been separately identified and years when they have been incorporated into the divisional figures. Producing an identifiable trend in profits over a reasonably long period of years does not always come easily from published accounts.

To summarise, it is a valid and necessary exercise to construct a profits model that can highlight the principal revenue streams, incorporate the relationship between fixed and variable costs, and isolate any significant elements of cost. However, the figures contained in group accounts will provide no more than an incomplete picture, which will need to be supplemented. Even then, such models will best work with one product businesses operating in the domestic market. Nearly all large companies have disparate streams of income which require forecasting separately and not as an amorphous whole. In those cases, the group accounts will contain no more than one line for turnover and one for profits and for these it is best to use multiple models – one for each element of the business.

Financing

Accounting issues present a problem for a book of this nature for there is no intention of, nor indeed any point in, replicating the legion of accounting textbooks and guides on how to use accounts. It is assumed that the reader of this book either has a basic knowledge of accounts and accounting issues, or is contemporaneously acquiring such knowledge. As has already been stated, the author's working assumption is that the accounts are a correct representation of the financial state of the company – in much the same way that a driving manual assumes that the car is in working order. Nevertheless, we must retreat marginally from this accounting disinterest to stress that, in reality, the corporate forecasting process cannot be disentangled from the accounts analysis.

The forecaster must always be asking whether the accounts conceal a reality that is significantly different from that which has been formally presented to the shareholders. Questioning the validity of the accounts may be outside the scope of this book but it is not outside the responsibilities of the forecaster. All that will be said here is that if a company appears to be making consistently higher profits than its competitors or than common sense would indicate is reasonable, then it may be that it has sustainable competitive advantages; alternatively, it may be that it has a market niche that is vulnerable to competition. It is at this point that the forecaster should be considering closely the third possibility – that the accounts are not as true or as fair as the audit report suggests. Although Terry Smith's *Accounting for Growth*[48] was not without its critics when published, it provides excellent examples of the way in which published profits could be favourably enhanced relative to their underlying reality. In commenting on his own screening system, Smith says 'it is only intended to pose questions, not to provide answers', an attitude that fits well with this book's approach to forecasting.

For practical purposes, this book stops at the level of trading profit; beyond that, the exercise is relatively mechanistic – interest charges and taxation have to be deducted and the earnings per share calculated. The inclusion of the interest charge, not

48 Terry Smith, *Accounting for Growth*, Chapter 5, 1992.

previously discussed, is the most critical factor, taking the forecast down from the operating to the pre-tax level. The balance sheet structure and the level of debt at the start of the forecast period are known, and assumptions can be made about probable changes in interest rates. For most companies, movements in the interest charge will do no more than amplify the changes that are happening at the level of trading profits; while it is satisfying to get the interest number correct, the reality is that the success or failure of the 'bottom line' forecast will be determined by the accuracy of the forecast at the trading level.

Having said that, there are companies where the level of debt is such that interest charges absorb a significant part of the trading profit; in other words, the interest charge does become material in a forecast of pre-tax profits. In these cases, the forecaster not only has to give serious consideration to probable changes in the level of interest rates (which, presumably, he has already been considering when making his assumptions about general trading conditions) but also to the future state of the balance sheet. In the short term, any significant change in fixed assets should be well signposted (the accounts note on capital commitments) so it is the movements in working capital that will require detailed attention. There is a fuller discussion of the relationship between the profit and loss account and the financing structure in Chapter 7.

Forecasting the unexpected

Implicit in the discussion of forecasting has been the existence of recognisable patterns of behaviour, or experience, that we can formalise and draw on. However, stating the obvious, we must never forget that we are dealing with the future and, by definition therefore, with the unknown. 'In forecasting, most errors consist of failure to anticipate untypical behaviour'.[49] The problem was more colourfully described by Christopher Fildes[50] as 'It's the alligator you can't see that bites you'. Events can arrive, if not necessarily out of the blue, at least with sufficient lack of advance warning as to make them appear to be near unforecastable. Indeed, the day after this paragraph was first drafted, the news of the Barings

49 Britton, A & Pain, N, *Economic Forecasting in Britain*, 1992.
50 *Daily Telegraph*, 10 January 1994.

collapse was announced. Speculative losses which have occurred during the 1990s include:

- 1991   Allied Lyons – foreign exchange;
- 1993   Metallgessellschaft – oil futures;
- 1994   Codelco – copper futures;
- 1994   Barings – stock market futures;
- 1995   Daiwa – unauthorised bond transaction;
- 1996   Sumitomo – copper trading.

But although they make the best headlines, sudden bad news is not just dealing losses; it also bedevils 'proper' businesses. Indeed, health scares might rival rogue dealers for their capacity to create immediate financial loss. A striking example was the government announcement in March 1996 that a link between BSE (bovine spongiform encephalopathy) in cows and Creutzfeldt-Jacob disease in humans could not be ruled out. This precipitated a collapse in not just the British, but the European beef market, with consequential effects on the associated trades – hamburger chains, gelatine manufacturers, etc. The *Daily Telegraph* reported[51] 'The little known Association of Cattle Head De-Boners which describes itself as one of the "Cinderellas" of the meat trade, says it was forced out of business without warning five weeks ago when the Government banned the use for human consumption of cheek meat from cattle heads ... more than 300 workers in 30 specialist firms lost their jobs as the plants closed.'

Three examples can be drawn from the pharmaceutical industry. In 1988 and 1989, the US Food and Drug Administration requested the withdrawal of two of Fisons' products – the company announced a year later that it had lost £65m as a result. Claims relating to silicone breast implants led to Dow Corning (the biggest maker of silicone) filing for Chapter 11 bankruptcy in 1995 and Bristol-Myers Squibb taking a $950m charge in 1996 to cover the costs of settling claims. And in the UK, in September 1997, the share price of the biotechnology company Biocompatibles fell 36% when it announced that the US healthcare group, Johnson & Johnson, had decided not to license its main product.

For a case of a company creating its own misfortune, one can turn to Ratners (then the world's largest jewellery chain) whose chairman gave a widely reported speech to 6000 members of the

51 27 April 1996.

Institute of Directors. How could they sell cut-glass decanters so cheaply? – 'because they are total crap'. A range of men's earrings was described as cheaper than a Marks & Spencer prawn sandwich – 'but I have to say the earrings probably won't last as long'. The immediate loss of public confidence that followed the widespread publicity given to those remarks turned profits of £112m into a loss of £122m the following year.

A more rational, but equally unexpected, corporate decision was that of Philip Morris in the USA to cut the price of its premium cigarettes by around 20% in April 1993 ('Marlboro Friday') in a move to regain market share from the discount brands (for the record, the share price fell 23% on the day). Three years later, when Philip Morris pursued the same strategy with its breakfast cereal prices, that decision was seen as a rational response to competition from much cheaper private-label products.

Although we can think of oil and mining exploration companies striking lucky, the nature of the completely unexpected is that it is more likely to be bad news than good news. Typically, dealing losses are compounded by people trying to undo previous mistakes so that a cumulative run of good profits ('proving' that the dealers must know what they are doing) is swamped by the one disaster. A drug can be put out of business overnight (though very little actually happens overnight) by the discovery of side-effects but the equivalent good news happens more gradually – a drug cannot be invented and brought to full-scale production in the same time period. A factory can be burnt down overnight but not built overnight. Or to take an everyday example, a one hour train journey can scarcely be more than a minute or two early, but it can well be more than an hour late.

Moving away from the completely unexpected, it can also be understood that it is easier for a company to fall short of a target than to exceed it. Production targets could well be set at 90 something % of capacity. It is not physically possible to do much better, but it is statistically possible to do up to a 100% worse. Or take a government project to build six hospitals; one can conceive of a shortfall in the target but even the most cynical observer of bureaucracy would be surprised to find that seven hospitals had been built. And so one could go on.

It may now come as a surprise to the reader if we suggest that there are forecasting lessons to be drawn from these examples. Perhaps the most obvious is really an aside: however successful a run you appear to be having with your profits forecasts, do not get cocky; you never know what lies around the corner. It matters little that the forecasting error could have been made by anyone; it was made by you, and anyone who acted on your advice will feel a touch irritated, however unreasonable that may appear. But, apart from advising humility, a rare characteristic for forecasters, what constructive lessons can be drawn – ▷**is the unexpected always unexpected?** ◁

⋈

The best that can be said is that there are certain types of business, and certain types of corporate strategy, that dictate caution. It would be unusual for the forecaster to be predicting, for one specific time period, an event that all other observers would regard as totally unexpected, and his strictly numeric forecast will typically be near (though not necessarily at) the mid point of his expectations. However, the advice or the decision making that accompanies that forecast will take into account the possibility of the 'unexpected' happening. This would explain why many individuals, without ever anticipating the timing of the insurance disasters that hit the Lloyds market, would not on principle have exposed themselves to that risk. Without necessarily being able to measure the risk, the forecaster should still be less surprised at 'unexpected' heavy speculative losses occurring in a company where such dealings are a part of its core business (they that take the sword shall perish with the sword), than if they surfaced in a manufacturing business that has no need of unmatched dealing on financial, foreign exchange or commodity markets.

The earlier comment referred not just to the risk inherent in particular industries but also to 'certain types of corporate strategy' and it is here that we may become aware of the potential for unexpected financial risk in what appear to be non-financial businesses. Let us take businesses that use large amounts of raw materials which are both specific to their business and an important part of their total costs – cocoa, coffee, wood pulp, PVC, etc. Large users of such commodities will have individuals or whole departments responsible for purchasing the commodities in the most effective way, which may be direct from the producer or on a commodity exchange. Moreover, there will be times when buying forward rather than spot will be more effective, particularly if there is a long production cycle and a requirement to fix both purchases and sales prices at the same time. Such hedging is an entirely prudent way to manage a business and, if the transactions are matched, entails no risk – only the possible loss of an opportunity to make abnormal profits if the selling market moves favourably after the purchase of the raw materials.

Now we come on to human nature. So far we have described a conventional purchasing operation, conducting itself efficiently and prudently. However, that purchasing department accumulates a considerable body of expertise in its particular markets and it is a simple matter to use that expertise to take advantage of anomalies that exist in the market. Routine purchasing then extends into (almost) risk-free arbitrage which of course, becomes a regular profit earner. The temptation to go further becomes irresistible and the department is no longer a cost to the business: the finance director establishes it as a profit centre with, of course, very tightly defined controls. That is the point at which the forecaster is entitled to say that there is more of a risk that the unexpected may occur.

How do we know that the company for which we are forecasting is conducting itself in this manner? Fortunately, human nature comes to the rescue again. The finance director, frustrated that he cannot run the proper business, now has his own profit centre reporting to him. It is probably making a fair amount of money – they always do at the beginning. And he is only too pleased to tell anyone who is prepared to listen, how successful he has been.

▷ **Beware the finance director who tells you that it makes commercial sense to develop his commodity purchasing, treasury (substitute as necessary) department into a profit centre, utilising their market expertise for the added benefit of the company.** ◁

Perhaps the 'unexpected' is more easily forecastable on the operating side of a business than for the more dramatic dealing losses. The drug industry was mentioned earlier and there are some companies where patented high margin products may represent a significant proportion of the company's total profits (in 1993, Zantac accounted for 44% of Glaxo's turnover and probably a higher proportion of profits; its world-wide market share was 38%). The forecaster should be acutely aware of the risk, whether judged probable or improbable, that the patent may be challenged or circumvented; that side-effects may be discovered; or an alternative superior treatment may be launched. He will know that the more profitable that drug is, the keener competitors will be to produce that 'unexpected' announcement; to some extent, the unexpected may be regarded as a 'when' rather than an 'if'. The forecaster will be doing his best to talk to as wide a range of people within the industry as possible and to be reading the trade and medical journals. ▷ **In practice, the totally unexpected may only be so for those who have worn analytical blinkers; to those forecasters with a wide range of sources, sensitive antennae and an ability to think laterally, the 'unexpected' may have been no surprise.** ◁

Significantly higher profits than are being earned by competitors, or by similar businesses, without any supporting industrial rationale can be an indication that risk is present. There were many who regarded the quantum of profit being made by Polly Peck from packing fruit in 'Turkish' Cyprus as inexplicably high. For them, the timing of the company's crash in 1990 may have been unexpected, but not the event itself.[52]

To take one more example of the supposedly totally unexpected, the UK electricity industry regulator announced in March 1995 that the five year price controls for the regional distributors, set in place provisionally only six months before, was to be reviewed – downwards. No better test of its unexpectedness was the immediate fall of around 20% in share prices and the hurried acceptance of and withdrawal of Trafalgar House's bid for Northern Electric. Yet what had preceded this unexpected announcement? A level of profitability in a regulated public utility sufficient to allow most of the participants to buy in their shares, culminating in a bid for Northern Electric, with the latter finding that it could return over £500m to shareholders. When, patently, excessive profits were being made; when those profits were being bid for by those in need of cash flow; and when those profits could be returned to shareholders; how 'unexpected' should it have been that the regulator decided that the bid for Northern Electric 'may have revealed new information about regional power companies' finances'?[53]

What is being described here is not, of course, an ability to predict the unexpected in its purest sense. Rather it is a description of what might be called, colloquially, being ahead of the pack; a description of the 'outsider' reading the Indian signs to get there a little ahead of his competitors. In the real world one does not need

52 One way in which commentators often implicitly assess the unexpected is by referring to the 'quality of profits'. High quality profits would be sustainable, reliable, derived from low risk areas. Low quality profits would, conversely, be perceived to have a high level of risk and be vulnerable to events outside the company's control.
53 Quoted in the *Financial Times*, 8 March 1995.

to be too far ahead of the rest to succeed as a forecaster. Indeed,

 ▷ **predict the demise of a best selling drug three years ahead and you will have a lonely time; predict it three months ahead and you will be a success; predict it three days ahead and you may be up for insider dealing.**◁

7 *The long term profits forecast*

Summary

The topics in this final chapter are not directly linked; their commonality lies in the time span. In the Introduction and in Chapter 2 on long term growth, we made it clear that our concern was not in the mathematics of a steady annual growth rate but more in the process of going ex-growth. This theme is continued with corporate examples taken from retailing and insurance and we show how publicly available statistics can clearly indicate the likelihood of future problems. We also look at the pattern of growth exhibited by high capital start-up companies, which exhibit different statistical characteristics.

One of the issues relating to growth is the means of financing that growth and we stress the importance of forecasting the balance sheet and, hence, the financing charges. Companies with a fast rate of growth in turnover and no more than a modest decline in operating margins can find that the cost of finance eats surprisingly heavily into the pre-tax profit.

The issue of long term scarcity, or the exhaustion of non-renewable resources, arises from time to time in the minerals industry and forecasters should be aware of the fallacies often inherent in what are often highly publicised 'doomsday forecasts'.

Chapter 7 concludes with a discussion on profits smoothing, an exercise often carried out by managements of cyclical businesses to make it appear that their particular company really enjoys steady profits growth. One sometimes wonders who is fooling who.

The end of the growth phase

Chapter 6 looked at profits forecasting within the framework of the short term cycle, the time frame within which most commercial forecasting activity is concentrated. However, many of the points made under the banner of cyclical forecasting – on model building, or on the way in which managements respond to external change – apply equally to long term forecasting. Nevertheless, there is a different emphasis attached to long term forecasts for the growth company and we would look particularly at two key issues. The first lies in the industry forecasting which was discussed at length in Chapter 2. Here, the forecaster is concerned not so much with projecting current growth rates as predicting when that growth will slow radically or even go into reverse. The second issue is the competition that fast rates of growth tend to encourage, and the irritating characteristic that growth markets have of attracting new competitors just as the growth is coming to an end. Interlinked is the nature of profit margins and return on capital employed in growth businesses.

There are some growth businesses that seem to return remarkably steady profit margins, year in, year out. They enjoy a stable environment in that there is no significant increase in the number of competitors. They will not be over-exploiting the opportunities that growth might offer, therefore in times of above average growth they will not be seeking to raise margins. Periods of recession probably mean no more than a slower than trend line rate of increase in sales. The unused slack in their pricing policy is available if required. On the cost side, it is much easier for a growth company to control expenditure by not increasing costs as much as it would have done (or at all), than it would be for a non-growth company to reduce costs. It is clearly easier not to take on additional staff, or not to lease an additional store, than it is to declare redundancies or hand back a redundant lease. Because we can understand and rationalise this corporate growth, there is a tendency to assume that it will continue if not for ever, then at least for the foreseeable future. The examples that follow have been chosen to demonstrate that the application of the thought processes outlined in Chapter 2 can provide clear signals of more difficult times ahead.

The retail industry

The retail industry contains some high profile growth companies, which have enjoyed both above average sales growth and steadily rising margins over a period of years. Tesco and Sainsbury have been among the leaders in developing ever larger food supermarkets and superstores. Their growth in market share has been conveniently set out in their accounts and Graph 7.1 shows how dramatic this has been. They have not been the only operators, of course, and Asda and Safeway have also increased their market share as has the slightly smaller Kwiksave.

In marked contrast, the smaller groups and the independents have lost substantial market share (Graph 7.2). It is this apparently inexorable growth in the large companies' market share that should immediately remind the forecaster of the discussion of saturation level in Chapter 2 where we saw that the mathematics of the S-curve made it difficult to sustain fast rates of growth when saturation had risen to around 35%.

It is not intended in these paragraphs to express any opinion on the prospects for the large superstores but to use them as an example of the way in which the industry statistics can signpost a slowdown in growth. Most, though not all, of the growth in the superstores' sales has come from the decline in the small retailer's position. With the market share of the independents, for want of a

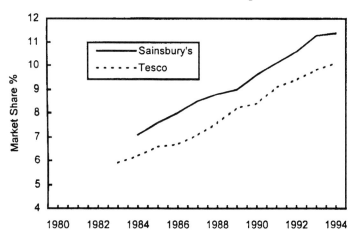

Graph 7.1 Retailers' market share.

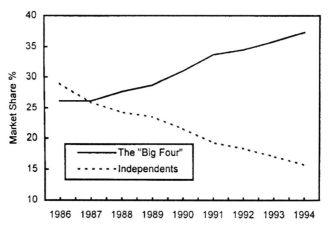

Graph 7.2 Retailers' market share (source: *Verdict Sector Reports*, Verdict Research Limited). Note: The 'Big Four' are Sainsbury, Tesco, Safeway and Asda; the independents are the small grocers and specialist food retailers.

better description, having halved to no more than 15% in the past ten years there was clearly not a lot left for the superstores to take. Market share can still increase but only at a slower rate. It is that slowdown in the rate of growth that begins to bring pressure on operating margins.

Having taken a view on the limits of growth in the food superstore market, we can then observe the trend of operating margins (Graph 7.3). Here again we can see consistent and substantial increases over a long period of years; this combination of increasing market share and margins has produced dramatic growth in operating profits. Our two food retailers, starting from low profit margins, have been able to reap the benefits of economies of scale and market dominance. Tesco's return on (average) shareholders' funds peaked in 1991 at 29% and Sainsbury's was also 29% in 1992, rates of return that are sufficient to attract new capital. Although the industry has not been characterised by new entrants, the existing companies have been competing aggressively for new sites.

Let us pull the strands together. It is always useful to start by recognising what it is that we do not know: we do not know what percentage of total food sales represents saturation level for the large superstores; and we do not know what the limits are to operating margins. However, we can see from the graphs that a further significant increase in market share must be

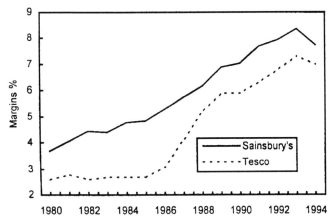

Graph 7.3 Retailers' operating margins.

mathematically difficult to achieve as the specific area from which that market share has been gained is now down to a low level. Much of that residual target market will be niche or monopoly outlets, perhaps in remote areas, serving customers who do not drive, or offering localised all-hours facilities. We can see that operating margins have steadily increased, producing returns on shareholders' funds that are high for a low risk business. And in this particular industry, forecasters have the added luxury of being able to look around them. (Thus, in the author's own locality, a London suburb of around 30 000 people, one modest Safeway has been followed by a Sainsbury's, a Marks & Spencer foodstore and a Waitrose with two more superstores being built on the outskirts, all within the space of a decade or so.) This is not the benefit of hindsight pointing to the problems experienced by the superstores in the mid-1990s with their intermittent 'price wars', nor a forecast of what may be to come. ▷**It is an illustration of the patterns of growth that are available to the forecaster and a message that he** **should be shouting out – this is what an industry looks like when it is going ex-growth: could it be happening here?**◁

In January 1994 Tesco announced a reduction in its store opening programme and a change in its accounting policy (to depreciating its stores and amortising its land premiums). The finance director specifically focused on the issue of saturation: 'Saturation of the market has been with us for some time, and what you are seeing is a continuation of that.'[54]

54 *Financial Times*, 20 January 1996.

Insurance

Another interesting example of rapid growth is provided by the 'direct' selling of insurance by telephone, without the use of broking intermediaries or an insurance company sales force. This particular area of the market was pioneered by Direct Line, the Royal Bank of Scotland subsidiary. Table 7.1 and Graph 7.4 show the share of the motor insurance market taken by direct insurers; unfortunately, the breakdown is not available for the years prior to 1990 but, as Direct Line was only formed in 1985, the rapid increase in the share of the market taken by direct insurers is self-evident.

The success of Direct Line within the sector it helped create has been well documented and Graph 7.4(b) compares the growth in total policies and profits. Graph 7.5 shows the growth in the total number of Direct Line policies outstanding for both its motor and household business.

There are a number of familiar characteristics to the growth profile of direct motor insurance in general and Direct Line in particular. There is a distinction between a new product or service that

- creates a market in its own right (the personal computer); or
- represents a different way of approaching an existing market without leading to any enlargement of that market.

Direct motor insurance clearly falls into the latter category; it is difficult to believe that the total number of motor insurance policies sold is any higher than it would otherwise have been.

Table 7.1 Motor insurance premiums (£m)

Annual premiums		1990	1991	1992	1993	1994
Industry	3080		3866	4317	5206	5201
Direct share (%)	12		13	16	20	25
Direct premiums	370		503	691	1041	1300

Source: Association of British Insurers: *General Insurance Sources of Business,* Table 2.

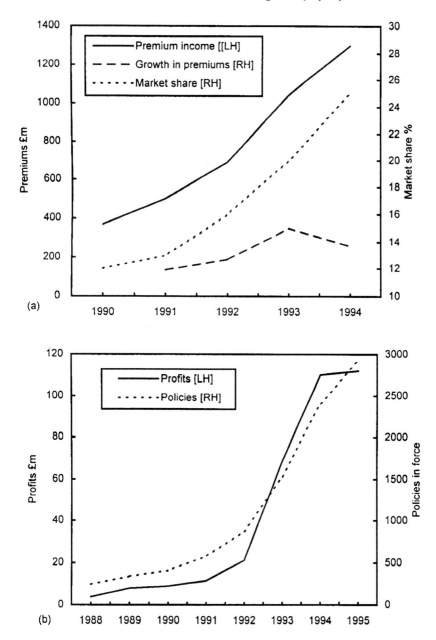

Graph 7.4 Direct motor insurance: (a) the industry; (b) Direct Line (source: Association of British Insurers). Note: Direct Line profits shown before Chief Executive's special profit sharing.

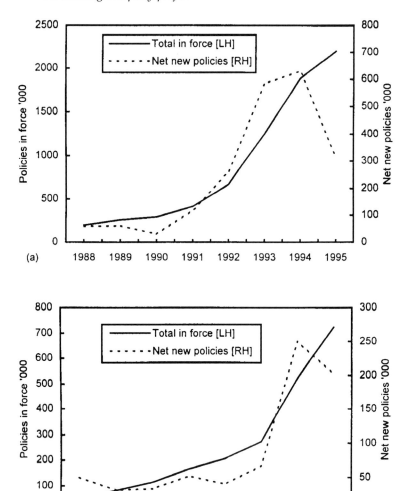

Graph 7.5 Direct Line policies: (a) motor; (b) household.

Given that the market only has to be attacked, and not created, it gave the new entrants all the advantages associated with cherry picking (discussed in Chapter 4).

- There was no historic baggage of out of date systems, thus enabling the new entrants to adopt the most cost-effective operational structure.
- They could target the lowest risk drivers and refuse high risk sectors. This is not merely a matter of expressing a preference

(much like investors who only want to select shares that go up in price) but having the ability and willingness to marginal price more tightly than the traditional suppliers of insurance and to react more quickly to changes in risk experience. Thus, direct insurers needed the computer systems to evaluate and price risk on a narrower basis; and the willingness to decline to do business with a large segment of the public. It is, of course, easier for a new entrant to decline to do business (either formally or by a discriminatory pricing structure), than for market leaders to chase away long-standing, if troublesome, customers.

If we return to our early discussion of saturation levels, we can see clearly from Graph 7.4 that, although the penetration of direct insurers had only reached 25% by 1994, the rate of growth in new business fell that year. Indeed, in surveying the direct insurance industry in August 1995, Market Assessment Publications stated that 'The sector has already virtually reached saturation point'. Direct Line itself had become the largest single motor insurer in the industry.

The final observation is that fast growth almost always tends to attract competition, thereby accelerating the arrival of individual corporate downturn. Indeed, new capacity often comes in at the point when the growth was about to stop. Thus, Direct Line was followed into the market by competitors such as Churchill Insurance (Winterthur) in 1989 and Admiral (the Lloyds Brockbank Group). All three were new businesses which added to the overall capacity and, hence, competitive pressure in the motor insurance market. Then the traditional composite companies, reliant on brokers and their own sales forces, began to react to the loss of market share by establishing their own direct subsidiaries, e.g. Guardian Direct, Royal Direct, G A Direct and Sun Alliance Direct. It is unlikely that there was an equivalent loss of capacity from their traditional operations; the composite insurers were also trying to reinforce their traditional links with the brokers that still supplied the bulk of their business at the same time as they developed direct selling arms.

If we take another look at Graph 7.5, we can see that although Direct Line's total number of motor policies continued to grow, the rate of increase declined markedly in 1994 and in 1995 the net increase in new policies actually halved. The inevitability of this slowdown, and the opportunity to apply the 'direct' principle in other markets led Direct Line into household insurance although the facing graph also shows this newer business segment experiencing a reduction in the rate of growth in 1995. To widen its business profile further, Direct Line entered the high risk sector of the motor market in 1994 through its Privilege subsidiary, and the whole life insurance market in 1995.

Direct insurance thus provides a classic illustration of rapid corporate growth within an existing, and mature, market. The pioneer, Direct Line, maintained a commanding lead over its imitators but once the direct sellers reached a quarter of the total motor insurance market, the rate of growth inevitably slowed. At the same time, the range of alternative suppliers was rapidly increasing, making the market more price competitive. The market leader responds by moving into other sectors of the motor insurance market, into non-motor insurance, and to overseas markets.

Sheltered housing

The sheltered housing market provides another example of a company targeting a specialist niche and then being faced with an upsurge in competition at the point where the market itself is going ex-growth. McCarthy & Stone had pioneered sheltered housing for sale in the 1980s, establishing a profitable growth record as a public company. Government projections of a rising elderly population over a 20 year period (see Table 7.2) were being widely translated into forecasts of substantial growth in the provision of sheltered housing to serve that segment of the population.

Two fundamental forecasting errors were made, both relating to concepts covered in Chapter 2. We said there that 'a basic error when looking at ownership statistics is to equate saturation level

Table 7.2 1985-based population projection: persons aged over 75

Year	1986	1991	1996	2001	2006
Households (000)	3602	3925	4098	4320	4391

Source: 1985–2025 Population Projections, Office of Population Censuses and Surveys.

with the maximum number of people or households for whom that product could theoretically be applicable, rather than for the much smaller number of people who actually have a requirement for the product.' We gave sheltered housing as a specific example when we said that 'forecasts … invariably concentrate on the number of elderly people above a certain age, rather than the far smaller number of elderly who both need sheltered accommodation and who are temperamentally inclined to choose it.' Thus, the first mistake was to overestimate grossly the potential market size.

The second mistake was the simple failure to distinguish between the rising population of elderly requiring sheltered housing (and hence the rising stock of sheltered houses) and the incremental increase in the stock of sheltered houses, i.e. new sales of sheltered houses – a return to our S-curve. By the end of the decade there were approaching 100 companies attracted into building sheltered housing; the phase of fast growth had been naturally coming to an end when the general recession in the housing market finished it off, and substantial losses were incurred.

On a practical note, there is an important difference between the first example on retailing and the third example of sheltered housing. That difference lies in the visibility of the statistics. If you look back at the retailing graphs, they clearly show that the market share of the majors was reaching a point where further growth would become difficult, and that operating margins had reached levels that were both high in historic terms and high in comparison with other retail or distribution businesses. No substantial part of the historic statistical framework had to be guessed – only interpreted. In contrast, the practical difficulty for sheltered housing was establishing one of key statistical building blocks – the real size of the market. The figures were there to show the theoretical four million plus elderly people, and even the proportion of those that owned their own houses – but not the considerably smaller number of people who would actually be the market. The forecaster therefore had to exercise what judgement he could on what the size of the effective market might actually be; to be aware of the pattern of the S-curve and its implications for incremental growth, and to be looking for any signs that the market might be reaching the critical point on that S-curve.

And one yet to come

The retail banking industry, as it stood in 1997, reminds us of many of the points that have been discussed so far in this chapter. A mature industry, controlled by a small number of very large businesses and earning high rates of return on equity, the retail banks themselves had copied the insurance sector by introducing 'direct' banking without waiting for an outsider to break in. Marks & Spencer had entered the financial services market as far back as 1987, steadily building up a range of financial services without ever offering full banking facilities. In the mid 1990s, major retail chains started offering simple cash-back facilities to customers paying at the check-out, following this up with customer cards offering limited deposit and cash withdrawal facilities. However, in March 1997, Sainsbury launched its 24 hour banking service; in June, Tesco announced its Clubcard product; and in October, Virgin also announced that it was entering the banking market. This is a classic example of cherry picking. Outsiders are using an existing retail structure to bolt on a carefully targeted range of low risk services. ▷ **If the reader is now nodding his head and saying 'I** ◁◁ **can see what is coming' then it will have demonstrated the opening comments about the importance of pattern recognition.** ◁

Perhaps it is appropriate to finish with another Warren Buffet quotation:

> Our equity capital is more than twenty times what it was only ten years ago. And an iron law of business is that growth eventually dampens exceptional economics. Just look at the record of high-return companies once they have amassed even $1 billion of equity capital. None that I know of has managed subsequently, over a ten year period, to keep on earning 20% or more on equity … the companies simply couldn't turn up enough high-return opportunities to make that possible.[55]

Another warning

Long term economic relationships are invaluable for providing convenient working assumptions and the base for speedy

55 Berkshire Hathaway 1985 Accounts.

forecasts; they are the received wisdom of the forecasting world. However, the more useful and reliable they are, the more dangerous they become when they break down. Examples of received wisdom (at the time of writing!) would be:

- expenditure on foreign holidays rises;
- rail travel declines relative to air and road travel;
- food expenditure falls relative to total consumer expenditure;
- computer software is a growth industry.

There is no more effective way of demonstrating the importance of checking that the received wisdom is, in fact, wise than by showing graphs (Graphs 7.6 and 7.7) of two economic truths that were prevalent in the 1970s and 1980s:

- cinema admissions are on a long term downwards trend;
- house prices always go up.

The cinema story is well known. Cinema attendance peaked in the late 1940s when it was one of the few cheap and socially acceptable ways of going out for the evening – or even, if I can remember my childhood, on a Saturday morning. A combination of a more affluent consumer base, a wider choice of alternative leisure pursuits, the development of television on the one hand; and a lack of investment in cinemas on the other, set in what appeared an inexorable decline in attendance. It is hard to identify what determines a social trend, whether an activity is 'in' or otherwise but during the 1980s investment in new cinemas[56] and aggressive marketing of blockbuster films began to make cinema going more acceptable which in turn produced more investment, with the results seen in Graph 7.6(b).

Post-1945 inflation carried house prices along with it; when 'real' house prices fell, as in the early 1970s, high general price inflation prevented nominal house prices from falling. Thus, nothing had occurred to challenge the received wisdom that house prices could only move in one direction. When the next substantial fall in real house prices occurred at the end of the 1980s, the low level of general price inflation meant that actual house prices had to fall, creating 'negative equity' for over a million house buyers.

56 The first Multiplex screen was opened in late 1985 in Milton Keynes and 10 years later such cinemas accounted for a third of all screens.

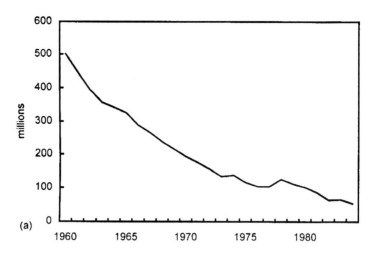

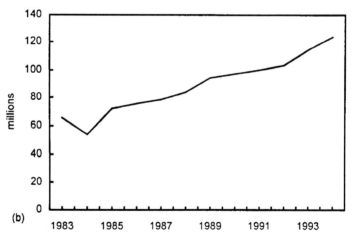

Graph 7.6 Cinema admissions: (a) long term decline; (b) the recovery.

High capital startups

The pattern shown earlier for food retailers is of margins rising from a point where new capacity is consistently being drawn into the industry to the point where over-capacity begins to occur, with resultant pressure on margins. An entirely different structure is found in the early stages of growth in capital-intensive businesses when the early years of development have to bear the costs of

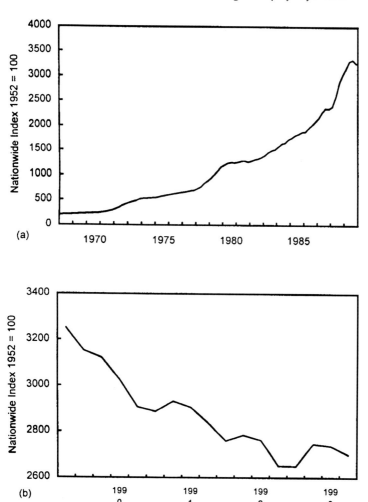

Graph 7.7 House prices: (a) house prices always go up; (b) negative equity (source: Nationwide Building Society).

creating an infrastructure. Although retailers may go through periods when they have an above-average number of new outlets coming on-stream relative to the overall size of the business, by and large they have the capacity to match their physical expansion to market growth. They had the advantage of being able to take an existing industry structure – small shops – and gradually modify it – to ever-larger shops. This ability does not exist for new products and services that have a high element of infrastructure. To some extent, this would have been a feature of Direct Line's early years. Extreme examples can be found in the communications industry – satellite and cable television; mobile telephones; Mercury's telephone network – but the principle is a common one. In these cases, demand may be growing rapidly but margins can be negative.

The introduction of satellite television into the UK involved high initial costs – primarily programming costs rather than the satellite itself. Indeed, the level of overhead expenses was such as to force a merger in 1991 between the two satellite companies. That merger blurs the financial information in the early years of the company's existence but Graph 7.8 clearly shows the emergence from operating loss into profit in 1993 and, after the high annual interest costs, into pre-tax profit in 1994.

As the cost of creating infrastructure slows down, or even levels off, operating margins will rise rapidly, thus providing the intended overall return on the project. Such a rise in profit margins is a normal feature of the product development process and should not, of itself, be taken as a danger signal. Detailed analysis needs to be made by the forecaster of the extent to which margins can rise before competition will be attracted.

Clearly, the more capital intensive the business, particularly when it is front-end loaded, the harder it will be for new entrants. But it is dangerous to assume that any business has such high capital costs of entry that new companies could never afford the entry price. BT, for example, had the protection of its national distribution network but regulatory changes allowing access to that network enabled Mercury to compete; on a more localised scale, cable companies are offering alternative telephone services to customers within defined urban areas. A regulatory insistence on access to distribution systems is also the means whereby the gas industry is being opened to competition.

Narrow monopolies can also be broken by near competitors. A UK Coal Board monopoly, strengthened by long term contracts with the Central Electricity Generating Board, led (without wishing to apportion blame) to a complacent attitude within the coal industry. Eventually, privatisation of the electricity industry, the need of manufacturing industry to obtain the lowest possible energy costs and the availability of cheaper oil and natural gas had their inevitable economic impact. It is not possible to play Canute indefinitely. Indeed, it is interesting to speculate what managements could consider themselves immune from competition. One

178

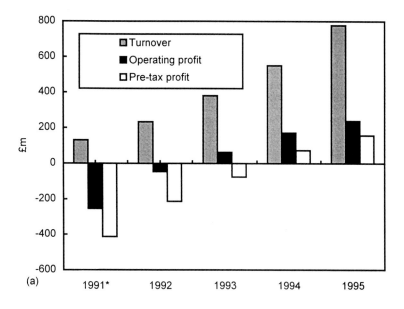

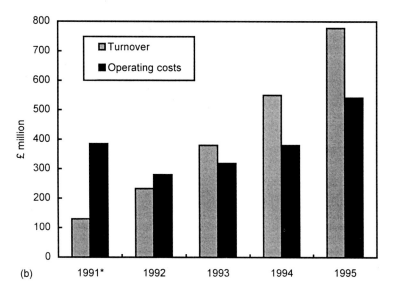

Graph 7.8 BSkyB television: (a) turnover and profit; (b) turnover and costs (*annualised figure based on 37 week trading year).

would probably come up with such examples as the water industry where it is difficult to imagine competition between the regional authorities, or even a ring of desalination plants around the coast. However, it is in precisely such industries that we find political interference in the pricing structure either formally through an official regulatory body or on an *ad hoc* basis.

Financing

We touched on financing, and interest rates in particular, in Chapter 6 and we suggested that, for most companies, the cost of finance was not likely to affect the forecast materially in the short term. In the longer term, however, the financing needs of a growth business become an integral part of the forecast. Table 7.3 shows a simple matrix that can take us through from sales, to capital employed, gearing levels and interest charge. Like most elements of the forecasting process, it can be made more complicated, though not necessarily to any additional effect.

There is a two way relationship between the balance sheet and the profit and loss account. The growth in turnover that is being forecast needs to be financed. A business enjoying real long term

Table 7.3 Financing profile

	0	1	2	Year 3 Forecast	4	5	6
Sales		100	110	121	132	145	160
Trading profits		10.0	11.0	12.1	13.2	14.5	16.0
Interest		1.7	2.0	2.3	2.7	3.1	3.6
Pre-tax profit		**8.3**	**9.0**	**9.8**	**10.5**	**11.4**	**12.4**
Taxation at 31%		2.6	2.8	3.0	3.3	3.5	3.8
Net Profit		5.8	6.2	6.7	7.3	7.9	8.5
Dividend at 2.5 cover		2.3	2.5	2.7	2.9	3.1	3.4
Retentions		3.5	3.7	4.0	4.4	4.7	5.1
Sales capital ratio	*1.5*	*1.5*	*1.5*	*1.5*	*1.5*	*1.5*	*1.5*
Capital employed	66.7	73.3	80.7	88.0	96.7	106.7	117.3
Equity capital	50	53.5	57.2	61.2	65.6	70.3	75.4
Debt	16.7	19.9	23.5	26.8	31.1	36.4	41.9
Net capital employed	66.7	73.3	80.7	88.0	96.7	106.7	117.3
Debt/equity %	*33.3*	*37.2*	*41.1*	*43.7*	*47.4*	*51.8*	*55.6*
Return on capital %		*15.0*	*15.0*	*15.0*	*15.0*	*15.0*	*15.0*
Interest at 10%		1.7	2.0	2.3	2.7	3.1	3.6

* The UK standard rate at the time of writing.

growth will have a requirement for additional fixed assets to support the increased sales, together with increased working capital – stock, work in progress and any excess of debtors over creditors.[57] Thus, once the forecast of trading profits has been made, there would need to be a parallel analysis of the means by which that growth is to be financed and the cost of financing. This will cover the forecasting of the interest charge and/or the impact of additional share capital on the earnings per share.

We can move through the table:

- The sales and trading profit forecasts are assumed to have already been made; in this case, the numbers are taken to be a simple 10% p.a. growth rate. The profit margins are assumed to be constant.
- A base year (year 0) is shown for the year end balance sheet; this equates to the opening balance sheet for year 1. We have assumed an equity capital of 50 and a debt to equity ratio of one third.
- The sales capital ratio is taken to be 1.5 throughout and is based on the annual sales and the opening capital employed (i.e. the previous year's closing capital). The ratio of 1.5 means that a given amount of capital produces sales of 1.5 times that capital or, alternatively, a given amount of sales requires capital of two-thirds of those sales. There may also be a case for separate forecasts of the sales to fixed capital ratio, and the sales to working capital ratio, especially if cyclical trends are being incorporated.
- The forecast of year end capital employed is derived by dividing the following year's sales by the sales capital ratio.
  The equity capital comprises the equity in the base year plus the annual profits retained after tax has been paid and dividends distributed; different tax rates or dividend payout ratios can be assumed as appropriate.
- Debt is a residual, being the required total capital employed less the equity capital.
- The interest charge is the year opening debt (i.e. the previous year's closing debt) multiplied by the assumed rate of interest. That interest charge is then deducted from trading profits to give pre-tax profits, thus feeding back into the balance sheet via retentions.

---

57 Debtors less creditors can, of course, be negative and therefore a source of finance.

This is all fairly straightforward with the aid of a simple spreadsheet – in fact, Table 7.3 is a straight copy of one. For those who actually want to construct such a spreadsheet there is one practical problem which is dealt with in the note below.[58]

Although the first objective of a financing model as in Table 7.3 is to provide a logical estimate of the interest charges, the exercise may also raise significant questions about the future structure of the business. The numbers used in Table 7.3 were chosen arbitrarily but intended to be not atypical of a modestly growing business. It is not until they are worked through that it becomes apparent that the balance sheet gearing rises consistently through the forecast period. If asked to guess the balance sheet implications of a 10% growth rate, 10% profit margins, a 31% tax charge, a dividend cover of 2.5 and a sales to capital ratio of 1.5, it would be an unusual reader who knew instinctively what would happen to gearing.

However, it is only when we begin to vary the assumptions that we appreciate just how sensitive the financing requirement can be. Table 7.4 presents an alternative financing profile, of a faster-growing business than in Table 7.3 but with profit margins coming under modest pressure over the five year period. Asked again for a quick reaction to a business growing at 15% a year but with margins falling from 10% to 8%, the response would probably be that the profit potential was good; indeed, at a trading level this is correct, with 60% growth over the five year period. However, the cost of financing the doubling of turnover produces sharply increased interest costs and leaves virtually no growth in pre-tax profits.

The forecaster now has a company where his assumptions have produced gearing approaching 100% and a business that epitomises 'profitless growth'. The objective behind Table 7.4 is to demonstrate the importance in a long term profits forecast of paying appropriate attention to the means of financing that growth, but what do you do when you get an answer like this? The first response, as always, is to check the assumptions – clearly, no

---

58 The pre-tax profit depends upon the interest assumption, which depends on the debt, which depends on the retentions, which depends on the profits. In constructing a model in this way, you will very quickly arrive at what the spreadsheets neatly call a circular reference and a lot of error messages. This can be avoided by entering approximate figures for the interest charge and, to put no finer point on it, 'fiddling it' until it works. Alternatively, as in this table, the interest charge can be calculated separately as a percentage of the previous year's debt, thereby avoiding circularity.

Table 7.4 An alternative financing profile

Year	0	1	2	3	4	5	6
				Forecast			
Sales		100	115	132	152	175	201
Profit margins %		10	10	9.5	9	8.5	8
Trading profit		10.0	11.5	12.6	13.7	14.9	16.1
Interest		1.7	2.3	3.1	4.0	5.1	6.5
Pre-tax profit		**8.3**	**9.2**	**9.5**	**9.7**	**9.7**	**9.6**
Taxation at 31%		2.6	2.8	2.9	3.0	3.0	3.0
Net profit		5.8	6.3	6.5	6.7	6.7	6.6
Dividend at 2.5 cover		2.3	2.5	2.6	2.7	2.7	2.7
Retentions		3.5	3.8	3.9	4.0	4.0	4.0
Sales capital ratio	*1.5*	*1.5*	*1.5*	*1.5*	*1.5*	*1.5*	*1.5*
Capital employed	66.7	76.7	88.2	101.4	116.6	134.1	154.2
Equity capital	50	53.5	57.2	61.2	65.2	69.2	73.2
Debt	16.7	23.2	30.9	40.2	51.4	64.9	81.0
Net capital employed	66.7	76.7	88.2	101.4	116.6	134.1	154.2
Debt/equity %	*33.3*	*43.4*	*54.0*	*65.8*	*78.9*	*93.8*	*110.7*
Return on capital %		*15.0*	*15.0*	*14.3*	*13.5*	*12.8*	*12.0*
Interest at 10%		1.7	2.3	3.1	4.0	5.1	6.5

management wants to double the size of its business deliberately to produce flat pre-tax profits and a weak balance sheet. But, if the assumptions about the rate of industry growth and the decline in margins still look the most reasonable expectation, what can the company do?

- The physical growth of the business may be restrained to within that which can be financed from the existing equity base but if the industry is fast growing and becoming more competitive, the company would still be suffering the lower margins.
- The payout ratio may be reduced (by the dividend not being increased) to increase retentions but this would make little difference in our example.
- There might be additional equity raised (a 'rights' issue in the case of a quoted company). A 1 for 2 rights issue would keep gearing down to 50% at the end of the period but earnings per share would actually be lower.

Which direction the management will take depends on a multitude of factors, its own temperament being not the least.

▷ **What is important for the forecaster is, first, that he realises that there is an inconsistency between his sales forecasts and the existing capital structure and, second, that he thinks through the possible consequences. This is fertile ground for the careful forecaster. In a fast-growing business most of the headlines will relate to the opportunities for growth and there will be a general air of optimism. Yet by working carefully through the numbers, the forecaster may be able to conclude that, at the bottom line, the return to shareholders will be quite different.** ◁

In a long term forecast for a growth company, the sales to capital ratio for fixed assets and for working capital may both be stable, thereby making it unnecessary to separate them out of a group sales to capital ratio. Although we are slightly out of our time context, we should make the point that in a short term forecast which is substantially dependent on cyclical movements, the two component ratios will inevitably differ and will need to be addressed separately. In most cases, the fixed assets will not be changing – on the upswing of the cycle, excess capacity will be absorbed; on the downswing, it will be created. The sales to fixed capital ratio is not a tool that will be used to assist a forecast, it will merely be derived from the sales forecast. The working capital sales ratio will behave quite differently and will require careful consideration. One can postulate a variety of scenarios which could include working capital moving, not in line with sales, as we saw in our long term model but in the opposite direction: thus, a recession creates an unwanted increase in stocks as sales fall; a recovery allows the increase in sales to be met, in part at least, out of stocks. There is no convenient rule of thumb that tells the forecaster what will happen to working capital requirements in a period of cyclical change.

Remembering that the sales to working capital ratio can be volatile does at least prompt the forecaster to think through the logic of what a company might be trying to do with its working capital and what pressure of external events may be forcing it to do. There are simple calculations that can be made to help the thought process: calculate what would happen to stocks if there was a 10% fall in sales without any corresponding reduction in production for three months. In other words, try to simulate what is happening to the relationship between sales and working capital and decide how the management might respond.

So far, we have been looking at the impact that the sales forecast can have on the balance sheet and how that reflects back on the profit and loss account via the interest charge. However, looked at from the other direction, changes in the balance sheet may also offer clues as to what may be about to happen to future sales. If there has been a major increase in fixed assets (perhaps accompanied by figures for future capital commitments) it is only done for a purpose – to generate future sales. That may already be evident from other sources, for instance, the directors' own description of their strategy. However, if the business is one that, historically, has had a stable sales to capital ratio, then there may exist a basis for converting that increase in fixed assets through to the sales forecast. An example might be an acceleration in a store opening programme. Alternatively, in a new business which is having to invest heavily in capital assets before sales can be generated, such as a television cable company, there may be precedents within other companies – at home or abroad – which would suggest an appropriate sales to capital ratio.

Long term scarcity

A recurring theme in long term forecasting is the prediction that, at current rates of growth, demand for this or that commodity will eventually outstrip supply. Such arguments have a lengthy pedigree. Malthus's *Essay on Population* (1798) argued that 'Population, when unchecked, increases in a geometrical ratio. Subsistence increases only in an arithmetical ratio'. As Malthus comments, 'A slight acquaintance with numbers will show the immensity of the first power in comparison of the second.' A forecast of a production shortfall, in this case of food, follows in a straightforward manner. This type of forecast, with accompanying pessimistic conclusion, was extended in the nineteenth century to raw materials and energy sources a favourite contemporary example being oil. (This branch of economics is sometimes referred to as the economics of non-renewable resources or exhaustible resources.)

The doomsday forecasts, as they might well be called, are most readily produced for resources where the international supply is well documented. Typically, there will be estimates of proven reserves, supplemented by probable or possible reserves. In other words, the forecaster will be able to quantify the capacity to supply. On the other side of the equation, the forecaster will also be able to measure the recent compound growth rate in demand. As long as that growth rate is positive, push the horizon out far enough and there will eventually be an excess of demand over supply. Obviously, the higher the recent demand growth rate, the shorter the time horizon needed to produce a shortage, which is why such forecasts tend to be more popular towards the end of a boom in world economic growth.

Without wishing to suggest that the doomsday forecasts can never be valid (the Kentish charcoal burners may have had a point), they do suffer from major fallacies. At the root of the problem is the comment made in Chapter 1, that forecasters have a preference for working with numbers that are available, and that can be modelled (preferably with some complicated mathematics), and less inclination to deal with the conjectural. We can immediately point to the two interlinked reasons why the doomsday forecast tends to be proved wrong, both of which relate to price movements and, in particular, the anticipation of future price movements.

One of the most comprehensive doomsday forecasts was *The Limits of Growth*, commissioned by the Club of Rome in 1972.

This study purported to show that on any reasonable assumptions of high rates of growth would mean that

> (i) the world would run out of resources of key materials; (ii) increasing pollution would have serious effects; and (iii) population would outrun the world's potential food supplies. This report was at first accepted by many sections of the public as constituting a scientific demonstration of the need for governments to take action to slow down growth rates.[59]

An increase in the relative price of a raw material will act as a restraint on the rate of growth in demand. There is a sense in which there can never be a shortage, merely an equilibrium between supply and demand at a substantially higher price than before. However, the common-sense view would be that there is a shortage of supply at prices that the consumers have been used to paying and would, indeed, be used to paying.

59 The New Palgrave *A Dictionary of Economics*, 1987.

Relative price rises will lead to economies in the use of the product both by reducing consumption of the service that the product provides (driving fewer leisure miles in the car) and to substitution by other products to provide the same benefit (power stations switching from oil to coal). This is how the demand curve is supposed to work.

On the supply side, a rise in the price of a resource also works to reduce the potential shortfall. Reserves that were previously considered uneconomic are now viable. Additional capital investment can be made to achieve a higher recovery of the product. But above all, a rise in the price encourages exploration for new reserves. 'The concept of "known resources" is a misleading one: society only "knows" of the resources that it is worth discovering given present and prospective demands, costs and prices.'[60]

The UK oil industry, which started production in 1975, provides a small-scale illustration of the way in which reserve estimates can be increased. The annual estimates of reserves[61] include identified oil fields, those regarded as probable, plus a further estimate for possible fields; in other words, they are not restricted to actual discoveries but include a reasonable estimate of what might be discovered. The figures in Graph 7.9 are the upper limit of the

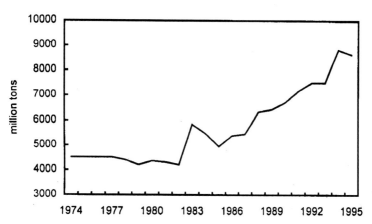

Graph 7.9 UK oil: initially recoverable reserves:[62] maximum possible estimate.

60 The New Palgrave *A Dictionary of Economics*, 1987.
61 UK Department of Energy: *Development of Oil & Gas Resources of the United Kingdom*; UK Department of Trade and Industry, *The Energy Report*.
62 That is adding back oil previously extracted.

187

range given for each year and it can be seen that, after the first few years, there was a progressive uplift in the estimate of maximum recoverable reserves. ▷ **In 1995, the maximum estimate of initially recovered reserves was nearly double the starting figure; indeed, after deducting all the oil produced over the 20 years, the maximum estimated remaining reserves were still 50% higher than the maximum reserve estimate before oil production started.** ◁

The comments above are critical of the doomsday forecasts but, to be fair, that criticism might more properly be directed at the way in which such forecasts are both misunderstood and misused. Ironically, the misuse of what are often no more than trend extrapolations has an important role to play in the market economy; the doomsday forecasts themselves are an essential part of the equilibrium process. They show what will happen if supply is not increased; they anticipate shortage and they therefore stimulate corrective action. Belief in the implications of the doomsday forecast may encourage research into more economic use of the resource or into the use of alternative resources – this would impact on the demand side of the equation. Anticipation of a shortage will also encourage exploration for new sources of the resource and means of improving the yield from existing reserves – thereby improving the supply side.

The objective of this section is not to suggest that all forecasts of shortage (relative or absolute) are fallacious. Rather, it is to ensure that the reader understands the limited premises on which many of these forecasts rest; to understand why many of the doomsday warnings are self-correcting; and to enable him to assess the extent to which the forecast may be self-correcting – in other words, to evaluate the forecast.

Much of the above comment on non-renewable resources could have been included in our Part I coverage of industry forecasting. But there are very particular implications when forecasting a company's profits. The forecaster must determine where the individual company stands in relationship to the supposed shortage: is it a producer or is it a user of the resource? If it is a producer of the resource (and here one thinks of the international oil and mining companies), the forecasting thought process will be conceptually simple and include underlying growth rates in demand; ratio of known and probable reserves to annual demand; demand and supply price elasticities; time taken to bring reserves into production, and so on. All these clearly relate to the discussion

Table 7.5

	Raw material	Cost of switching raw material	End-product
Not vulnerable	Easily available alternative(s)	Low	Difficult to substitute
Vulnerable	No easily available alternative	High	Easy to substitute

above and the role of the forecaster will be to assess the importance of these factors for the relevant resource – a well-documented area.

However, entirely different considerations come into play if the company whose profits are being forecast is not a producer but a user of the resource. In this case the question is, can it easily substitute another raw material without affecting the saleability of its own end-product? We can envisage a matrix of conditions, relating both to the raw material, and to the end-product (Table 7.5); this can be used as an aid to thinking about the impact of both short and long term resource shortages.

Smoothing profits

We finish this book with a digression on an aspect of profits forecasting which rarely finds even a mention in the literature. What are we forecasting – the profits that the company actually makes or the profits it discloses in its accounts? This comment is not directed at the relatively few companies that fraudulently produce accounts showing non-existent profits but at the vast majority of companies that believe it to be in the shareholders' interests to smooth out commercial life's ups and downs.

Indeed, one of the characteristics associated with growth companies is this consistent upwards progression of profits. It is still argued in the public arena that investors prefer the comfort of a smooth (and, of course, upwards) profit record to one that is cyclical; above all, nasty surprises are to be avoided. The inevitable response has been profit smoothing, usually built on conservative accounting in the good times to provide a cushion for both the inevitable lean years and to meet the unexpected. How this can go wrong, we see below.

The investor relations psychology can alter the timing of profit upturns or downturns relative to the real results. If a company thinks it has sufficient profit reserve to cushion it through an anticipated profit downturn then it will use that cushion to hold profits. Once management reaches the conclusion that the severity of the downturn is such that profits are bound to fall at some stage in the future, then the temptation is not to use the cushion and get the profits fall out of the way. If that change in expectations takes place after the end of the financial year, then the 'guidance' given to financial analysts at what would be regarded as a late stage in the year (even after the year end), can prove surprisingly wide of the mark.

The same psychology is also observable in taking provisions against assets, be they land holdings in the property development business, or textile work in progress, or banking bad debts. If the downturn in values is perceived to be short term in nature then there will be an incentive to 'sit it out'; however, once it is accepted that a provision against existing values is inevitable, the emphasis switches to making the provision immediately and even indulge in a degree of overkill to get all the bad news out of the way and prepare for a speedier profits recovery. It was a measure of the severity of the downturn in the early 1990s that many finance directors had to indulge in overkill in two successive years.

Profits declarations coming out of a recession will also be subject to their own psychology. After the first 'artificial' bounce in profits (artificial in the sense that it will merely reflect the absence of provisions and other exceptional charges), recovery in published profits will tend to lag behind the recovery in profits actually earned. Managements will be concerned to rebuild their inner financial reserves and it may be that the particular traumas associated with the 1990–92 recession induced a financial over-conservatism that colours the whole of the 1990s. In that event, the best lead indicator for a period of above average growth in profits might not be industry statistics but the appointment of a new (and young) finance director.

We end with an example, well familiar to the author, of a company that produced unbroken profits growth in what must be one of the most cyclical industries – Taylor Woodrow – which was used as an example in *Construction Equities: Evaluation and Trading*.[63] Taylor Woodrow had suffered a sharp setback to profits

63 Woodhead Publishing, Cambridge, 1994.

190

in 1960 but from then onwards the profits movements were upwards for a period of almost 30 years; generations of City analysts came and went without ever seeing a downturn in the company's profits. Within the component parts of the business, the expected cyclical fluctuations did occur with the overseas contracting profits in particular being feast and famine. A closer examination of the individual subsidiaries' accounts at Companies House during this period would show that whenever there was a sharp change in overseas profits, coincidentally there was a countervailing movement in the profits of the UK contracting company which could lead the outsider to deduce that a policy of smoothing was being practised.

With the 30th record year of growth in prospect for 1990, we now know that it was not to be. Along with the other contracting majors, profits collapsed and a loss was incurred in 1991. The interesting question is, were there signs available that would tell the outsider that whatever it was that had prevented profits falling in the previous 29 years was no longer going to work? If not, then any pretence at profit forecasting might as well be abandoned.

Even without the benefit of hindsight (or perhaps just a little) there were signs, not necessarily of the extent of the fall that was about to happen, but at least that the composition of Taylor Woodrow's profits flow was quite different from what it had been even ten years previous. The property activities had been progressively expanded since Taylor Woodrow Property was formed in 1964 and the rental flows actually increased the stability of group profits. However, during the 1980s, Taylor Woodrow became more active as a seller of property and in 1985 it changed its accounting policy to include profits on the sale of investment property, previously taken as an extraordinary item. By 1989, 40% of group profits came from the sale of investment properties; throw in profits on development properties and private housing at the top of the market and the figure rose to 66%. In contrast, contracting profits only accounted for 14% of the group total: the property tail was wagging the contracting dog, and even with the best will in the world, no finance director could create contracting provisions that would be large enough to act as a regulator of group profits. Anyone taking the view that property and housing were cyclical businesses would conclude that a fall in profits was likely. The Taylor Woodrow example emphasises the importance of a full understanding of the structure of the company for which the profits forecast is being made and provides a final reminder ⋈ ▷ **that what has always been does not necessarily continue.** ◁

Conclusion

It has been suggested that, having explained the intricacies of forecasting, the book should finish with a worked example neatly illustrating all the points covered. It would be a pleasing way to end but no single case study would encapsulate the variety of themes that have been developed (and separately illustrated) throughout the book, and this is especially true given the different requirements of cyclical and long term forecasting. Unfortunately, the real world is not neat. However, it might be appropriate to finish with, if not a formal conclusion, then at least a few comments.

If there has been a common thread running through the book it has been the importance of 'pattern recognition', first mentioned at the opening of Chapter 1. The need for pattern recognition was predicated on the fact that even the professional forecaster does not have the time to prepare, or have access to, all the data that in an ideal world he should be using in his forecast. In relation to his subject, he is an outsider. On the well-worn premiss that it is better to be roughly right, then the book has concentrated on showing the reader roughly what happens in a range of frequently found industry and corporate situations – different types of cycles, going ex-growth, niche markets – and why it happens.

In the author's experience, many of those at a senior level in industry (and, let it be said, not excluding professional forecasters) do not recognise some of the most important of these patterns, even when they are staring them in the face. Interestingly, even when these patterns are recognised, if they represent a potential deterioration in trading, or a limit to potential growth, there may still be a reluctance to face up to the implications – hence the plea implicit in the subtitle of the book: 'this time it will be different'. Forecasters seem happier dealing with good news – perhaps they can make more money retailing it, perhaps it just makes them feel better.

There is a rule in investment advice – know your client. The equivalent rule in forecasting should be – know your company. We have dealt with the sources of information on companies but we want to go deeper than the mere amassing of information: to be colloquial, we want to know what makes the company tick. How does the company behave during cycles; how far up the ownership curve are its products; does it depend on a rising population for its business or are its sales based on the incremental change in a population; is it a weak player or a strong player in its market segment; are there barriers to entry; can it control its own destiny, and so on.

Forecasting should be a questioning process. We are dealing with economic flows, industry trends, company structures and the reactions of ordinary people to the consequent changes. From all this we distil what we think is a range of potential outcomes and, finally, we put a number down on a piece of paper. At the end of the day, we must always ask: does this number look sensible. Is it a surprising result; if it is, might some of my assumptions be faulty? If it is a forecast of sharply deteriorating profits, might managements be able to take some form of preventative action – and if so, at what stage? If the forecast is for a period of rapid profits growth, do the answers produce returns on capital that are likely to prove unsustainable? Might the status quo be challenged by new entrants? However, if you are as satisfied as you can be that your thought processes are still right, then stick to your forecast. The one final requirement for the successful forecaster is to be able to keep his nerve when all around are saying he is wrong and, let it be said, to have a thick skin.

▷ **'The best I can hope for is to be intelligently wrong or fortunately right'[64]** ◁

---

64 Anon, from *A Dictionary of Economic Quotations*, 2nd edn, compiled Simon James, 1984.

Bibliography

Bails, D G and Peppers, L C, *Business Forecasting Techniques and Applications*, 2nd edn. New Jersey, 1993.

Britton, A and Pain, N, *Economic Forecasting in Britain*, 1992.

Holden, Peel and Thompson, *Economic Forecasting: an Introduction*, Cambridge, 1990.

Hogg, Neil, *Business Forecasting Using Financial Models*, Pitman, London, 1994.

King, J A, *Foundations of Corporate Success*, Oxford, 1993.

Kotler, P, *Marketing Management*, Prentice Hall, 1998.

Livesey, F, *Economics for Business Decisions*, London.

Makridakis, S and Wheelwright, S C, *Forecasting Methods for Management*, 5th ed, New York, 1989.

Paulos, John Allen, *Innumeracy Mathematical Illiteracy and its Consequences*, Penguin, Harmondsworth, 1990.

Saunders, J A, Sharp J A and Will, S F, *Practical Business Forecasting*, 1987.

Smith, Terry, *Accounting for Growth*, 1992.

Wellings, Fred, *Construction Equities: Evaluation ad Trading*, Woodhead, Cambridge, 1994.

Projections of Households in England to 2016, Stationery Office, 1995.

1991-based National Population Projections Series PP2 no 18, Stationery Office, 1993.

Annual Abstract of Statistics, Stationery Office.

General Household Survey.

Guide to Official Statistics, Stationery Office.

Regional Trends, Stationery Office.

Social Trends , Stationery Office.

Monthly Digest of Statistics.

Financial Statistics.

Index

Sectors and products index

198

Companies index